Whether you choose to fix healthcare or not, the job is yours! Healthcare **cannot** be fixed by Washington, by self-styled experts, or by adopting some other country's system.

There are too many special interests. The power of inertia seems overwhelming. The issues are emotional, contentious and polarizing. Worst of all, those with power see all solutions in terms of political compromise.

Imagine your doctor saying this. *I have negotiated with everyone. I can remove part of your tumor but have to leave the rest. Your cancer needs four drugs. The pharmacy and I have reached a compromise: you get two.*

That is obviously ludicrous. Yet that is exactly what happens when political solutions are applied to medical problems. Politics is the "art of the possible." What U.S. healthcare needs is the necessary.

You and only you can, must, and will fix healthcare. This book is your guide.

Uproot U.S. Healthcare

"He *must* be there."

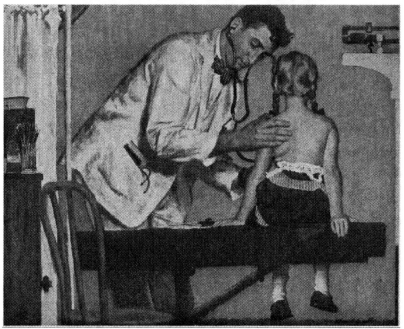

This work is dedicated first to the nurses, doctors, therapists, administrators, housecleaning staff, maintenance crews and all others who toil in the world of healthcare for the betterment of others.

This book is also dedicated to the *patients* and to my family, from whom I have learned so much, but only a beginning about how we can all help each other.

Uproot U.S. Healthcare

To Reform U.S. Health Care

Deane Waldman, MD MBA

ADM Books, Albuquerque, NM

Order this book online at www.uproothealthcare.com.
or at www.bookmasters.com.

Cover art by Banu Alpay (www.banualpay.com).
Figures & graphics by Paul Akmajian (pakmajian@salud.unm.edu)

Printed in Ashland, Ohio.

ISBN: 978-0-9827268-0-8 (sc)
ISBN: 978-0-9827268-1-5 (e-pdf)
ISBN: 978-0-9827268-2-2 (e-pub)

Library of Congress Control Number: 2010905194

*ADM publishes books that improve our individual lives and
promote social change through dialogue.
Please visit ADM online at www.uproothealthcare.com. and at
Deane's personal blog: www.thesystemmd.com.*

ADM rev. 04/13/10

ADM Books
Albuquerque, NM

Printed by:
www.bookmasters.com.
Phone: 800-537-6727. ♦ Fax: 419-281-0200.

Prologue

Every one on earth has a terminal condition…called **life**. We all want to make it as enjoyable as possible (be healthy) for as long as possible (live a long time). The system called healthcare is supposed to make that happen but is failing. Indeed, its sickness is making us sick. Many people have tried to fix healthcare but have made things worse. It is time for something different. We need to step back, open our eyes, and clear our minds.

In the past hundred years health care *technology* has made astonishing progress. Healthcare *thinking* has been stagnant. Healthcare providers work in the 21st century. Healthcare planners, economists, regulators, and managers are mired in the 19th century. The healthcare system simply isn't…a system. We need to uproot old thought and replace it with new thought. We need to look at things differently. We need to learn and put down healthy roots.

Learning is our most important decision aid (Chapter 1). It begins by discarding old, linear thinking (Chapter 2). Modern health care is a process, a series of systems, many of which are holdovers from times past. The medical malpractice system is one such and in Chapter 3, we uncover why it does not work – why it is a *malprocess*.

You, me, every one: we are all "thinking systems." Chapter 4 shows why this new concept is critical to both understanding healthcare and to fixing it. People–the 'parts' of a thinking system–act in accordance with their deep-seated values. Chapter 5 explains what drives health care people–their culture. All conversations about healthcare either start with or quickly settle on the money. This is called the pocket nerve (Chapter 6) and while money is an important incentive, it is not the only one that affects how people behave. In Chapter 7, we explore the relationship of incentives (rewards and punishments) to behaviors and finally to outcomes.

Healthcare has the perverse habit of measuring (Chapter 8) only the outcomes that patients do *not* want. In Chapter 9, we start to practice *good* medicine by diagnosing our sick patient: healthcare.

Chapters 1 through 9 are <u>de</u>scriptive or diagnostic. Chapters 10-12 are <u>pre</u>scriptive: offering treatment plans we must implement in order to get what we want. We start by changing how we think, as shown

1

in Chapter 10. By changing our mental models, we will change what we do–our behavior (Chapter 11). Behaviors determine outcomes. So changing behaviors will change outcomes. Chapter 12 describes how we can change healthcare to create a system that works for us.

This Book's Title and H.R. 3590

I wrote a book titled "Uproot Healthcare" before H.R. 3590 (also called "Obamacare") was passed. I had naively thought that since Congress called what they were doing "reform," their Bill would create change for the better. I was wrong. If you are someone who ardently believed that H.R. 3590 would fix healthcare or simply someone who hoped that it was at least a start in the right direction, it won't and it isn't. H.R. 3590 is the opposite of reform. It is exacerbation: it will make healthcare worse.

Though H.R. 3590 actually has little impact on what I initially wrote, it was clear that any discussion of healthcare had to include references to its supposed "reform" embodied in H.R. 3590. The book you are holding is called "Uproot <u>U.S.</u> Healthcare" to distinguish it from the earlier (pre-H.R. 3590) book called simply "Uproot Healthcare."

As the reasons for healthcare 'sickness' remain unresolved, and the symptoms become worse under H.R. 3590, you will need this book more than ever. As you read, you will begin to understand why the new law is what doctors would call *practicing bad medicine*. It temporarily palliates a single symptom and makes the other symptoms as well as the whole patient worse. It leaves the causes of sickness untouched. It is as though a doctor 'treated' a patient with cancer by giving her morphine. Congress has failed as a healer of medicine. Now you must do it.

You Are The Doctor (Or Will Be)

Whether you want to be the doctor for healthcare or not, the job falls in your lap. Washington has been guilty of malpractice and made healthcare sicker. Some who understand this are urging that we simply adopt some other country's "universal" health care system. As you will learn, others' solutions will not work here.

Part of the reason for Washington's failure is the old saw: when all you have is a hammer, everything looks like a nail. For people in Washington, all answers are and must be political.

Imagine your doctor saying the following to a cancer patient. (I keep using a cancer analogy because healthcare truly has a potentially fatal condition.) "I have negotiated a nice compromise with the nurses' union, the insurance agent and the electrical company. We have time to remove part of your tumor. I will have to leave the rest in there for an operation later." Of course that is ludicrous. Yet that is exactly what happens when politics are applied to medical problems.

Good politics makes bad medicine. Healthcare is sick and needs a country doc not a savvy negotiator. Political answers are always watered down by compromise and re-election mania. Politics may be the "art of the possible" but what we need is *the necessary*. Fixing one part of one organ or compromising with cancer is bad medicine and just won't work.

Acknowledgements

Until I wrote this book, I did not appreciate how much support and understanding authors need from others. No one ever writes a book alone. To Dana and Wade but especially Mary–my apologies, thanks and love.

To my colleagues in healthcare at all levels and to my patients, I again offer my respect and thanks.

We *Always* Learn

Whether we are alone or we are in groups, _humans always learn_. It is in our nature. We may learn the wrong things, like how to smoke cigarettes. We may learn things that are false, like smoking is good for you. [1]

In this chapter:
- How do we improve *anything?*
- Process of learning
- Special issues
- Get what we want

We may learn that to survive by avoiding making decisions and taking no risks. We have no choice *whether* we will learn–we will. We can choose *how, what, and why.*

Healthcare does not have all the answers and to find those answers, providers need to learn. How did healthcare find out about infection, diabetes, or leukemia? By learning. If we want cures for breast cancer, Alzheimer's, rheumatoid arthritis, or how to provide high quality health care services with limited resources, healthcare must learn.

How Do We Improve *Anything*?

How do we improve anything? Answer: *by learning.* In the dictionary, to learn means to acquire knowledge of or skill in [something] by study, experience or being taught. The strict definition of learning should be amended to focus on improvement. The person new to bicycle racing is taught proper pedaling action and cadence. The novice rider practices that motion and rhythm over and over until it is smooth, efficient and delivers the most power to the pedals. The surgeon-in-training learns how to incise the skin, enter the abdomen, identify the structures, control bleeding, and remove a diseased gall bladder.

Assuming that the cyclist always rides on the same flat terrain and that all people with an inflamed gall bladder are identical, the behaviors that were perfected by practice will always work. But, what if the cyclist must climb hills? What if next patient's gall bladder is in an unusual location? The new situation requires adaptation or change. More important, might there be a new better way–one not invented yet–to ride a bike or to remove a gall bladder? Twenty years ago, there was no such thing as removing a gall bladder through several tiny incisions and twenty years from now, it will be probably done without surgery at all.

4

Process of Learning

In *The Fifth Discipline* Peter Senge wrote that we all love to learn. Organizational behavior expert Edgar Schein [2] took an opposite position writing, "You can't talk people out of their learning anxieties; they're the basis for resistance to change, none of us would ever try something new unless we experienced the second form of anxiety, survival anxiety–the horrible realization that in order to make it, you're going to have to change."

Whether we learn because we like to or we learn simply to survive, humans always learn. It is our unique characteristic that we can learn with intent and with specific goals. No other "system" can do that.

Systems and Learning

There are three types of systems: Machine; Complex Adaptive; and what I call thinking systems (that's us), explained in Chapter 4. Any machine, from a plow or to a super-computer, does what it is programmed to do. Machine systems do not learn by themselves.

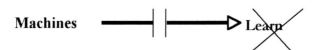

Much has been written about complex adaptive systems (CAS). [3] Forests and beehives are complex adaptive systems. Machines cannot learn. They produce predictable outcomes. A CAS can learn and produce unexpected outputs. The process by which a CAS learns is random rather than directed to a specific outcome. A CAS learns for only one purpose: to improve survival.

Contrast a flock of birds to the mass (peloton) of riders in the Tour de France. Over millennia, birds learned to fly in a V-shaped formation, constantly rotating the lead position. The bird up front does the most work breaking the wind while the others slipstream behind resting until their turn at the front. In this manner, birds can travel further and faster to survive till their destination. No ancient imaginative bird genius set up a series of experiments to determine the best flying formation. Birds did not pre-specify what outcome they wanted. Evolution drove them to co-evolve, self-organize, and learn how best to fly with species survival *emerging* as the outcome.

The Tour de France peloton looks like a flock of migratory birds. The cyclist at the front works very hard for a brief period of time and then slips back into the pack to recover. In this way, the peloton can maintain average speeds of 24-29 miles per hour for hours!

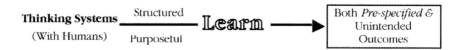

Months before the actual Tour de France, each bicycle team begins to experiment. They test which team members are better at climbing versus sprinting; which bicycle frame is more efficient on which stage; the best order of riders in line; and optimal aerodynamic position and even clothing. All these activities are *structured learning* aimed at multiple pre-specified goals. Only humans can structure their own learning. In activities like healthcare, where guaranteed *answers* are not known, structured learning is vital. Otherwise, we will never get answers.

Learning with Purposes (Plural)

Machines do not learn. Complex adaptive systems learn to survive, the end point being sex, well, procreation. Thinking systems like you, me, and the organizations we work for, typically want to survive (and have sex), but thinking systems always have *multiple* purposes – some may be more important to them than survival. Recall what the New York City Firefighters did on 9/11. [4] The ability of thinking systems to have multiple different outcomes complicates how learning should be structured. Do we want to focus our learning on better health treatments or on spending less money? The answer is both. To do this, we must understand the process of learning.

Types of Learning

Thinking systems can learn three different ways: Rote learning; Practiced variations; and Innovation. The first is a prerequisite to the second. Only the third can produce improvement.

Rote Learning

After someone teaches you how to serve a tennis ball, you practice. First, you only occasionally make contact with the ball. Then you learn the right angle of the racquet to make the ball land on the opponent's side of the net. Continued practice makes you able to place the ball within the service area every time. Eventually, with arduous practice, you can make the ball land in different parts of the service area, with different speeds and even with a kick or curved bounce after landing. This is a result of rote practice.

Rote practice allows the physician to diagnose conditions quickly and accurately. Rote practice allows a surgeon to remove a gall bladder in under two hours. Rote practice perfects your ability to do the same thing over and over with the same results...*assuming the conditions and the desired outcomes* are the same every time. What if the conditions are not always the same? What if the desired outcome changes?

Practiced Variations

A second type of learning is practiced variations, such as airline pilots in their simulators. Pilots first practice the rote actions of starting an airplane, take-off, flying and landing until they can do this the same way every time. Despite the fact that experienced pilots have done start-up procedure thousands of times, each *next* time, they do not depend on memory but use a printed checklist. In medicine and surgery, start-up checklists are still inexplicably rare.

After the pilot has mastered the rote procedures, he or she practices variations. What if conditions are icy? Practice icy take-off and landing in a simulator. What if you are flying through a hurricane? Practice flying in a hurricane. What if the hydraulics fail and you cannot lower the landing gear? It seems best that the pilot *not* have to learn how to deal with this, as a first experience, with us in the plane!

Flight planners think up every situation that they can imagine and pilots practice those variations. As passengers, we can board with confidence that the pilot has practiced every conceivable situation. But what if the plane encounters a new–not previously conceived and therefore never simulated–situation?

Innovation

Innovation strictly means to "introduce something new; make a change in something established." I prefer to use the word innovation more broadly to include the creation phase, the step of creating (not just introducing) something original. Sir William Bragg, 1915 Nobel laureate in Physics said, "The most important thing in science is not so much to obtain new facts as to discover new ways of thinking about them." Bruner's definition of creativity captures the essence: "Figuring out how to use what you already know to go beyond what you currently think." [5]

For over 100 years, investigators have studied how innovation occurs, how it diffuses into the general knowledge base, and is adopted. [6] A necessary precursor to innovation is the person's mindset: open, not certain of his/her correctness, willing to consider silly, *obviously wrong*, and/or unpopular ideas. A second pre-requisite is an environment and culture that encourages new ideas and risk-taking. Modern health care is the antithesis: there is a great deal of rote practice, some practice of variations, but innovation often gets stopped before it gets started.

Unplanned Versus Structured

You can learn just by doing, without planning either how to learn or what to learn. Simply by driving to work every day, you learn traffic patterns and the quickest routes versus the shortest distances. Most of what we learn is unplanned.

Our employer does not intend for us to learn *not* to take a strong public stand on a controversial issue (apologies for the double negative). Our manager does not intend for us to learn that there is only one right way to do things. However, that is what most workers learn. They learn quickly or they get terminated: unplanned learning of unintended lessons.

Learning can and should be structured for both the process and the outcomes. In medical school, there is a necessary sequence of learning steps, each step planned to build on previously acquired knowledge.

You must learn anatomy before you can study surgery. You need to learn how nerves work before you can understand nervous conditions.

The method of learning, the order of things learned, and testing what was learned–these things can all be planned. The old Bell Telephone repairman had to learn about electricity and switches before he was allowed to climb up the pole to fix the line. [7]

Who Can/Should Learn?

Individual persons can learn, indeed are forced to learn by their nature. Individuals in groups–organizations, industries and nations–can learn but may also choose *not* to learn.

Individuals

I can just hear you say *some people refuse to learn*. Not true. They are human. They always learn. Some have learned that something new is too threatening for them. Therefore, they enshrine the status quo of their current knowledge. These are people who do not adapt, will never improve, cannot innovate, but they *have* learned.

Sometimes we learn things we do not want to learn or things that change our worldview. These are the hardest lessons. They require unlearning.

In 1975, I had an experience that radically changed my view of medicine, indeed changed my life. I wish everyone in health care could have been there.

In my sixth year of training after medical school, I was studying Pathology at a very prestigious medical center. I had been there just a month when I performed an autopsy on a child who had died after complex heart surgery. I was the lowest academic position possible: Instructor. The man who operated was a world-renowned surgeon. I had to present the autopsy findings before approximately 75 physicians of various rank (all higher than mine).

Haltingly, I projected pictures of the heart with incisions, patches, tubes, etc. and carefully avoided giving any Cause of Death. After about ten excruciating minutes, the surgeon stood up and said the following. "Dr. Waldman, I do not know why you are beating around the bush. This child had complex double outlet right ventricle of a type I had never seen before. I misunderstood the anatomy, sewed the patch so that it prevented blood flow into the lungs. As a result,

9

he died." He then sat down. One of the greatest surgeons of his time had just said, in public, that he killed a child! I was literally speechless. When I eventually sorted out this event, several things became apparent that I have never forgotten and need to share.

Firstly, the surgeon took responsibility for his acts. He made a decision (what angle to sew the patch), he made a mistake, and the child suffered. Secondly, he certainly meant to help the child, not harm. The problem was his, indeed all our (then current) understanding of such complex heart problems: our knowledge was incomplete. Thirdly, he learned from that act, especially because he was willing to see what he had done and was willing to accept responsibility. He would never make that mistake again. Fourth, because he accepted this openly, the rest of us **learned** two things: 1) the details of the anatomy in this child, and 2) the behavior that he modeled: hide nothing, look at all outcomes, accept the consequences of our decisions and *learn* from them to do better in the future.

A recent medical malpractice case demonstrated the exact opposite. In a premature baby the patent ductus arteriosus (PDA)–a vessel widely open in all babies in the womb–failed to close after birth and need surgical closure. The surgeon mistakenly tied off the artery to the left lung (LPA) instead of the PDA. The family sued.

At pre-trial discovery, this surgeon accepted no personal responsibility. He claimed that he did nothing wrong. A representative series of questions and responses is offered below.

Question:	Did you do the operation on Baby X?
Answer:	I was the primary surgeon.
Question:	How did the ligature [tie] get on the LPA?
Answer:	A ligature was placed on the structure in proper position for the PDA.
Question:	Who did the operation, you or your assistant?
Answer:	I did, with his help.
Question:	So you tied off the LPA instead of the PDA?
Answer:	The procedure was performed without technical error. I did nothing wrong. The anatomy was incorrect.
Question:	Did you intend to close the LPA?
Answer:	I performed the operation correctly. Ligation of the LPA is a reported complication of surgery on the PDA.

In a technical legal sense, both surgeons committed manslaughter: "the unlawful killing of a human being without malice aforethought." Actually, both performed surgery with goodwill aforethought. Who learned: Surgeon #1? Surgeon #2? The healthcare system? Who would you rather as the surgeon for your child? Does our present healthcare system encourage learning?

Organizations

As individuals, humans always learn. As groups, they often do not. Most organizations including hospitals meet a commonly accepted definition of insanity: they do the same thing over and over, and expect different results. It is fascinating that this definition of insanity basically says that if you do not learn, you are insane.

Suppose a hospital first tried Reengineering; then six months later tried TQM (Total Quality Management); and six months after that, they started TPS (Toyota Production System). Nothing changed. What have they learned? They think they learned is that Reengineering, TQM or TPS does not work. Wrong. They should have learned that cultural changes takes years sometimes decades to demonstrate results.

By far the most difficult act for most organizations is a cultural change, such as to encourage learning. The company must celebrate the outlier, the one who is different. The culture must consider "different" as potentially good rather than automatically bad. There must be visible, tangible and *positive* consequences to risk-taking. 3M company requires that 25% of their profits be derived from products less than 5 years' old. This means their people must innovate new things if they want bonuses. At 3M, doing what worked before is *dis*couraged in order to promote learning.

Industries and Political Entities

Status quo (non-change) is the opposite of innovation and learning. The power of status quo grows in proportion to the number of parts in any system, from one person to a whole organization or hospital, to our nation. The more people involved, the harder it is to challenge accepted wisdom.

Success fosters confidence and confidence encourages mental rigidity. It is much harder for the CEO of a hospital to change his mind about what is right than for a nurse. The CEO *knows* that what he knows works. After all, he succeeded in ascending to the top of the corporate ladder. The same is true of countries. Those that have been successful continue on their current course. *Why should we learn and change? What we are doing works!*

Many social scientists and change agents believe one must apply the *burning platform theory* to large organizations. They say the only reason an authority figure gets off his platform (with its microphone) is when it is burning. Thus, to affect change, set the platform on fire.

Special Issues in Healthcare

Healthcare has four unique constraints to learning and to unlearning: 1) The substrate; 2) The external environment; 3) Worker retention; and 4) Culture.

Remember in high school when we had to add vegetable oil to a strong alkali? The oil was the **substrate** and the reaction, called saponification or soap making, produced glycerin and soap. When Gary Klein developed the aluminum bicycle frame, the substrates he tested were tubes of varying caliber and wall thickness to see which was best. The vegetable oil, alkali and aluminum bicycle tubes were the *substrates* – the things, elements or parts on which the system acts. In healthcare, the "substrate" on which the providers learn is us and we do not like being guinea pigs.

In the chemistry lab, the oil never rejected the alkali, but patients often refuse to do what they are advised. There is no natural shortage of bauxite to make aluminum tubes but there are less than 1000 patients in the country with identified metabolic disorders of the heart.

Ethics plays no role when you make soap in chemistry lab or when you test tubes for bicycles. It plays a large role when you consider testing on humans or on animals. Ethics is a real and highly appropriate constraint on learning in healthcare.

The **external environment** imposes a series of constraints on what providers can do to learn, each intended to eliminate risk. Regulatory prohibitions and bureaucratic restrictions have a huge damping effect on the ability to test anything. Some are appropriate but many are not. Look at David Dilt's flow chart on page 152 to see the latter. Taking *any* medical risk is strongly discouraged even prohibited, though the disease itself may have dire risks for the patient.

Risk management in most hospitals does not focus on reducing risks for patients. Their primary focus is to reduce the institutional risk of a lawsuit. Because of Risk Management's stringent interpretations of rules, regulations and guidelines, hospitals constrain not only research and learning but even medical care.

The public expects answers to medical problems. The environment–representing you the Public–behaves as though such answers are known and enshrined in standard procedure. When adverse outcomes occur, someone *must* have failed to follow procedure and the environment punishes someone. But answers are not known; results are not predictable; and when the medical system tries to do better by learning (taking risks), this is punished or severely constrained. The environment–legal and regulatory–aggressively protects the status quo and actively discourages learning.

Over the past thirty-five years, the aviation industry has developed a safety-conscious culture and process that has undoubtedly saved thousands, possibly hundreds of thousands lives. [8]

During a brainstorming session with two ex-NASA engineers, we were discussing some of the problems in the healthcare world, especially related to learning. They were shocked to learn the way healthcare handles errors, negligence, mistakes, malpractice, or adverse impacts–whatever you want to call them. They described the investigations that occur after a near miss or a crash. I countered with how healthcare treats a mistake just like an abscess: wall it off. The engineer exclaimed, "Are you guys crazy? We *always* learn from each others' accidents."

Learning takes time. In healthcare, it takes lots of time. If the workforce keeps churning and **retention** stays low, there is not enough time to learn. Imagine a medical student who keeps moving from one school to another every month. Would you want that person as your doctor?

Being a good doctor or nurse takes more than knowledge of anatomy and physiology. There are a host of factors not in books related to the specific work environment, hospital or office, that you need to master if you want to give effective and efficient care. Who does digoxin levels here? What kind of tube do I need? How long does it take? Where do I find and how can I read a chest x-ray on Mrs. Jones? Who should I call at midnight to admit a patient? Which technician is better at what?

To acquire this information takes time-on-the-job. Only after you learn can you consider a possibly better way [unlearn]. Then, you must learn how someone tries something new. With half the doctors staying where they are less than five years and with 83% of nurses leaving their current institution within five years, [9] learning in healthcare is prevented and innovation is stopped.

The culture of healthcare (Chapter 5) is extremely risk-averse and discourages learning. While this is partly in response to a hostile external environment and over-regulation, part of the problem also lies within healthcare. In order to improve medical outcomes, cultural elements that encourage learning should be elevated and anything that restricts learning should be eliminated.

Volume-to-Outcome Relationship

We have had proof that volume affects outcome since the 1936 paper titled "Factors affecting the cost of airplanes." The more you do, the quicker you get. In business, this means the more you do, the cheaper it becomes.

In medicine, multiple reports demonstrate a very strong positive relationship between volume and results. [10] Low volume is associated with more adverse outcomes. The data is not as clear regarding cost savings but there too, greater volume produces efficiencies of both scale and scope.

Learning Curve Theory

The three simple theorems that form the basis of learning curve theory have been verified in diverse activities from violin-making to heart surgery. Though learning curve theory is widely accepted and used in business, it has yet to make inroads in healthcare. [11]

Theorem #1 says the unit production cost goes down as the number of units produced goes up. In other words, the more you do, the quicker you get. Since time is money, the quicker you are, the less the cost. ↑ **Volume** → ↑ **Outcome.** In medicine, this means the 100th patient will have a quicker and safer operation than the first.

Theorem #2 says that the improvement achieved with increased volume *decreases* over time. This means you can never be perfect. This makes sense because if the improvement simply continued forever, eventually you could do something in no time, literally. With practice, you can get quicker when building a car or transplanting a heart, but you will never do it in zero minutes.

The third theorem states that improvement-with-experience follows a predictable pattern–it is neither random nor general. While violin-making, auto manufacture, and heart surgery all have learning curves, each activity has its own curve of a specific length and shape. You can predict and improve learning *by structuring the learning process*.

Feedback Loops

Fickeisen and other learning theorists [12] have shown that structured learning can focus the learning experience on specific outcomes and thereby improve (left panel in Figure that follows) our thinking or cognition. By improving cognitive function, learning itself is enhanced. This is a positive feedback loop, one that helps us improve whatever we are doing.

A positive feedback loop means that it constantly increases itself. Not positive feedback loops are 'positive' in their outcomes. A nuclear explosion is a positive feedback loop. The earsplitting screech you get when a microphone is too close to the amplifier is another undesirable positive feedback loop. Most learning generates desirable or useful positive feedback loops.

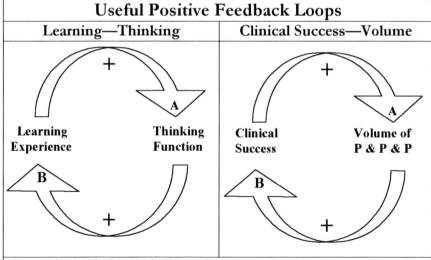

Useful Positive Feedback Loops

Learning—Thinking	Clinical Success—Volume

Curve (A) begins the loop and (B) completes it. [+] Means that the curve increases where it is pointing. P & P & P = patients & providers & payers.

15

To have a highly successful medical program in say cancer or heart disease, an institution must create a process that is effective and compassionate for patients, efficient for payers and attractive to providers. Any program with satisfied patients, payers and providers becomes: a magnet for more patient volume; a place where providers choose to come and stay; and a facility with which payers choose to do business. As the volume of all three P's increases, outcomes improve. **Increasing a person's experience starts a beneficial positive feedback loop, mediated by learning.**

Learning To Get What We Want

To reduce medical errors; to have better (anything) than what you have now; to assure specific desired outcomes, *we must promote learning*. That is the reason for this belabored discussion of how healthcare learns or does not.

Unfortunately, the current system is extremely risk-averse, which tends to suppress learning. Furthermore, starting with HIPAA and now H.R. 3590, the primary emphasis of healthcare regulation is information security. Easy and rapid exchange of information is curtailed even prevented. This reduces the ability to learn. Everything possible must be done to reverse this priority: learning should come first and security added afterward not the other way around (as is now).

To begin learning, we first must understand cause and effect in healthcare and how logic is often substituted for evidence. We need to stop thinking in straight lines and **use causal loops.**

Broken Loops

In our everyday world, we expect cause to be connected to effect and the person who 'acts' is the person who causes the result. Not so in healthcare where the outcomes are *disconnected* from the people who make them happen.

In this chapter
• Logic is not enough.
• Unintended consequence
• Lines and loops
• Using evidence
• The Figure-of-8 loop

Logic Is Not Enough

Every waking minute of every day we make decisions. Do I need a new tube of toothpaste? What should I wear? Is my report ready for the committee meeting? What should I buy for our wedding anniversary? What would make this sick patient well?

We make decisions for one purpose: to solve problems such as: enough toothpaste? Staying dry; satisfy the boss? Have a happy spouse; making a sick person well. A good decision is the first necessary step to solve a problem.

Making good decisions requires clear understanding of what we want as well as what is possible; judgment to choose among various options; and an effective decision making process. The process may be as simple as feeling the tube of toothpaste or as complex and formal as government flow charts, balance sheets and legislative subcommittees.

Logic and reasoning are our primary tools for decision-making. Unfortunately, they are often the *only* tools we use. As science fiction author David Weber quipped in all seriousness, "Logic is sometimes a way to err with confidence."

Oxygen–the breath of life. Without it, the cells in your body do not work. Deprived of oxygen for the length of an NBA time-out and your brain is damaged. Try holding your breath for just one minute and you can feel your body screaming "Breathe!! I need oxygen." Logic and past experience of our bodies for millions of years tells us that oxygen is good; without it, you die. How could oxygen possibly be bad for you?

That is what everyone thought, including doctors. They reasoned that if low oxygen is bad, then high oxygen must be good. Makes sense, logical, and in several situations, it is completely wrong. In adults, we now know that high oxygen can be toxic to the lining of our lungs. In infants with a specific congenital heart problem (hypoplastic left heart syndrome), oxygen can divert the blood away from the body into the lungs and cause death. In premature babies, breathing high oxygen can damage the baby's immature eyes causing blindness.

Our initial logic–that oxygen could do nothing but good–seemed impeccable. We learned the hard way about oxygen toxicity: by having patients suffer. Logic is not enough.

There is no question that cocaine is bad for you. If cocaine is harmful to an adult, would it not be even more dangerous for a fragile, developing fetus inside a pregnant woman? Since the fetus is affected by everything the mother eats and breathes, even her moods, taking cocaine should definitely be harmful. It constricts blood vessels and reduces blood flow to vital organs, especially the developing fetal brain. So, medical advisory warnings were issued, trainees in Pediatrics were taught the dangers of cocaine in pregnant women. This made sense and was quite logical. There is just one problem. The data does not show a significant danger when babies of cocaine-addicted mothers were studied! [1] Logic is not enough.

In addition to logic, we all use intuition to make decisions. Psychologists tell us that intuition is another form of logic, just below conscious level. *Intuitively obvious* is often used as the explanation, or should I say the excuse, for doing something. In many cases, by the use of evidence, intuitively obvious is subsequently proven to be dead wrong. Remember that when someone starts a sentence with "Everyone knows that…" or "It's *obvious* that…," they are saying something widely accepted that may well be wrong.

For important decisions, such as those involving patients, *intuitively obvious* gets us into more trouble than it is worth.

Intuitively Obvious Is Often Wrong.

It is intuitively obvious that:	*BUT:*
Stomach ulcers are caused by acid.	Micro-infection is a primary cause of ulcers.
Cocaine is bad for a fetus.	Follow-up data shows little-to-no damage.
Women should stay in bed for 5 days after delivering a baby	Tell that to millions of Chinese who immediately return to the fields.
Medical information must be protected at all costs.	All costs? What if the cure is worse than the disease?
Shrinking tonsils reduces throat infections.	Shrinking tonsils with X-rays causes thyroid cancer.
You must stay at strict bed rest for 4 weeks after a hip replacement in order to let the joint heal.	Getting up and moving improves healing and prevents a pulmonary embolus (blood clot in the lungs).

The Unintended Consequence Was Death

The case described below is a dramatic example of an unintended consequence (death) due to insufficient evidence and improper feedback. The natural inclination is to blame a person and indeed there was a lawsuit claiming medical malpractice. However, the real culprit is the system.

A teenager with chest pain during exercise was referred to a pediatric cardiologist. After a full work-up, the specialist thought the boy either had a normal heart or had a rare condition where one coronary artery (that supplies blood to the heart muscle itself) was in an abnormal place: a coronary artery might run between the two great arteries where it does not belong. If so, pulsations of the two arteries with exercise could block coronary flow and cause chest pain, even death.

The cardiologist decided to do a non-invasive test first, an MRI (magnetic resonance image) before doing an invasive cardiac catheterization. The official MRI interpretation by the radiologist read: "No abnormalities detected." The cardiologist thought this meant the coronaries were normal, cancelled the invasive test and allowed the boy to go back to sports.

Two years later, the teenager died suddenly while playing soccer. At autopsy, the coronary problem originally feared by the cardiologist was found and presumably caused the demise.

The family sued both the radiologist and the cardiologist and won. The truly guilty party is the system: guilty of failure to produce evidence and failure to accomplish effective feedback.

All actions are intended to solve a problem. The cardiologist was not just doing a consultation or ordering a test or even trying to see the coronary arteries. His *problem* was that he wanted to assure that chest pain was not a sign of danger. If the radiologist had the same goal, there would have been better images and/or clearer communication. He would have written something like: "The central coronary arteries cannot be seen. The coronaries further out appear to be normal." Had this been done, the cardiologist would have proceeded with the invasive study, found the problem, recommended surgery and the child would be alive today.

The family won their lawsuit and presumably the doctors were chastised. Did assigning blame and punishing the perpetrators prevent the same unintended consequence from happening in the future to someone else? Of course not: the system did not learn.

Lines And Loops

The linear thinker follows the great Sir Isaac Newton who saw the world as a giant, complex machine with cogs, pulleys, and levers. A first cause prompts an action that has a consequence. Thus, an assembly line worker [the cause] tightens a bolt in a car [the action] attaching the wheel to the axle [the consequence]. This produces a straight line between cause and effect.

Cause → Action → Consequences [end, finish, over]

The word "consequences" is plural because a single action never has just one consequence. Before examining feedback and multiple consequences, consider the everyday example below.

Linear Thinking in Action

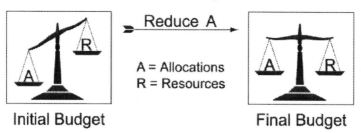

A = Allocations
R = Resources

Initial Budget   Final Budget

20

A manager might have an out-of-balance budget with more allocations – requests for money – than there is money or resources. By eliminating some of the allocations, the linear thinker balances the budget. For example, [New Mexico] "Governor Richardson's administration is proposing a 3.4 percent reduction in payments to health care providers in order to help slow the growth of Medicaid spending." This creates a balance between the supply of money and the needs of sick people by reducing the resources available for care. It that the balance we want?

Systems thinking, to be described later, is a highly useful way to look at the world and to solve the problems we encounter, whether personal, organizational, or even national. The central thesis is that all, repeat *all*, outcomes we experience in life are the result of interactions, not of isolated or linear actions. The pictorial representation of systems thinking is the causal or feedback loop.

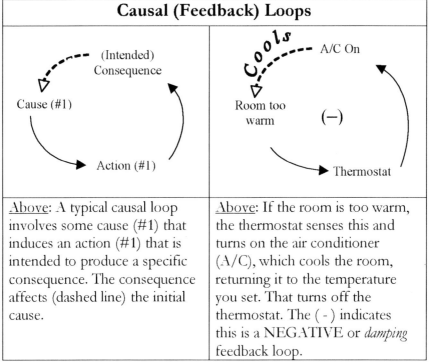

Causal (Feedback) Loops

Above: A typical causal loop involves some cause (#1) that induces an action (#1) that is intended to produce a specific consequence. The consequence affects (dashed line) the initial cause.	Above: If the room is too warm, the thermostat senses this and turns on the air conditioner (A/C), which cools the room, returning it to the temperature you set. That turns off the thermostat. The (-) indicates this is a NEGATIVE or *damping* feedback loop.

Though we undertake an action expecting a certain effect, most actions have multiple effects: some expected and some surprise, some pleasant and others not so pleasant.

Once you make a decision, there are innumerable and unending ripple effects. Some you can see. The majority of effects are unseen and in the future. You can begin to see how such loops play out in everyday life, very much including healthcare.

In healthcare, there are so many examples of unintended adverse consequences that I had difficulty choosing just one. Consider the Health Insurance Portability and Accountability Act of 1998, abbreviated HIPAA. [After pronouncing "HIPAA," most healthcare providers turn and spit, or make a sign to ward off evil spirits.]

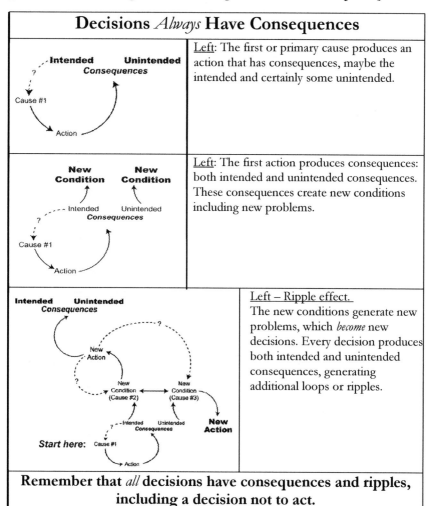

Decisions *Always* Have Consequences

Left: The first or primary cause produces an action that has consequences, maybe the intended and certainly some unintended.

Left: The first action produces consequences: both intended and unintended consequences. These consequences create new conditions including new problems.

Left – Ripple effect.
The new conditions generate new problems, which *become* new decisions. Every decision produces both intended and unintended consequences, generating additional loops or ripples.

Remember that *all* decisions have consequences and ripples, including a decision not to act.

HIPAA was conceived to address a serious problem experienced by American workers. Because of organizational restructuring and RIFs (reductions in force, also known as layoffs), people often lost their medical insurance when they lost their jobs. The "P" in HIPAA stands for the word portability. In conference discussions leading to the legislation, someone asked about transfer of medical information when moving insurance. It was agreed that confidentiality must be protected. The Act provides punishment for any breaches in the confidentiality of medical information. *There was no evidence that a significant problem ever existed.*

The intended consequence–portable health insurance–never happened. Unintended consequences followed

(A) Hospital lawyers, trying to protect their institutions, created rules to protect confidentiality that constrain the ability to transfer any medical information (unintended result).

(B) Another likely but yet to be proven (clearly unintended) consequence of protecting medical information is an increase in medical errors. Pharmacists are now forbidden to make known certain classes of drugs to treating physicians! Thus, the primary doctor may not know that *his* patient is taking an anti-depressant prescribed by a psychiatrist.

(C) Lawsuits are being filed claiming *either* that vital medical information was inappropriately withheld or that sensitive information was inappropriately released.

(E) The cost of medical care has increased by hundreds of millions, possibly billions, of dollars. As the cost of HIPAA does not appear on any budget sheet, it is another addition to the list of unseen but very real costs of regulatory compliance and unfunded mandates.

HIPAA provides an excellent example of a broken loop due to the lack of evidence and feedback. Without them, no system of any kind can be stable, much less improve itself. Our entire healthcare system is one big broken loop.

Loops that are broken

We live in a market-driven economic system and believe that competition produces better quality at lower costs. Suppliers compete or consumer dollars. Consumers reward the best supplier with money, "best" being defined by what consumers consider the best *value*.

The public, most of our legislators, and many self-styled experts believe that competition between hospitals or healthcare systems will weed out those with bad medical outcomes or who waste resources. That is what the US marketplace does well, certainly better than central economic planning, which brought Russia to collapse. All we have to do, they say, is unshackle market forces and let them work.

Unfortunately, the usual market forces do not work in healthcare because the supply–demand (microeconomic) *loops are broken.* To understand broken loops, first consider an intact one.

An *Intact* Supply-Demand Loop

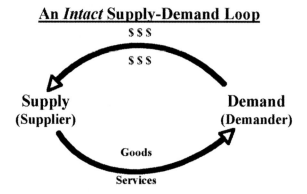

Figure above shows an intact loop: supply affects demand and demand affects supply. The supplier makes goods or provides services for demander (consumer) and consumer rewards the supplier/provider with money. If the volume or quality of what is supplied gives goes down, the reward (money) also goes down. If you apply that concept to healthcare, you will see that the loop is broken, as shown below.

A Provider–Patient (*Broken*) Loop

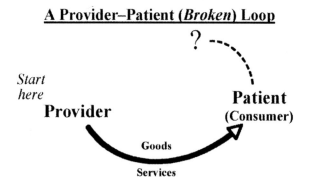

In health care (prior Figure), the provider gives goods and/or services to the consumer (patient) but there is no equivalent feedback from patient to provider. It is unclear to whom the patient gives any feedback. This open or broken loop is called micro-economic disconnection: where supplier and demander are disconnected from each other. In healthcare, what about the payer?

A Provider–Payer (*Broken*) Loop

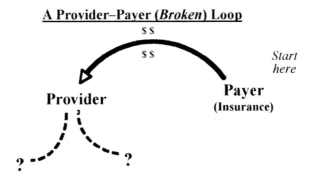

The payer–insurance company or government–gives money to the provider but the amount of this "reward" is regulated and has no relation to the quality, volume, or speed. This loop is as broken as the provider–patient loop in above Figure. Whom does the provider give feedback to?

Finally there is market competition. Car manufacturers compete with each other for consumer dollars based on price, features and reliability. Providers A and B–doctors, hospitals, or vendors–compete based on what? Certainly not anything the patient (consumer) wants. The payer rewards (with dollars) based solely on price and definitely not anything the patient (consumer) wants. The *market* in healthcare makes no sense and does not work because all healthcare micro-economic loops are <u>broken</u>.

Using Evidence

The Practice Of Medicine Is Evidence-Based…

Evidence is "that which tends to prove or disprove something." The word is commonly used in both healthcare and the law but with a fundamental difference: the time horizon. In legal proceedings, whether criminal or malpractice, evidence is used to determine what happened in the past. In medicine, evidence is used to predict what will happen in the future.

One hundred years ago, medical *cures* were hocked on the street by word of mouth with success **guaranteed** in a stentorian voice by the carnival barker-like dispenser. Homeopathic and osteopathic physicians vied to see who could heap more vitriol on the other. George Bernard Shaw, who hated doctors with amazing passion, heaped some of his finest insults in the Preface to *The Doctor's Dilemma.* [2] "As to the honor and conscience of doctors, they have as much as any other class of men, no more and no less. And what other men dare pretend to be impartial where they have a strong pecuniary interest on one side? Medical science is as yet very imperfectly differentiated from common cure-mongering witchcraft." While 19th century investigators in the natural sciences were using rigorous scientific techniques, doctors were emulating a used car salesmen.

Over the past century and despite unique difficulties applying scientific methods to human illness, practitioners of medicine have begun to accept their obligation to evidence-based decision-making. They are becoming more scientist and less salesman.

The phrase "evidence-based medicine" can be attributed to A.L. Cochrane, [3] who emphasized randomized, double blind, placebo-controlled trials as the cure for bias, intuition and latest personal experience. The practice of medicine is moving toward evidence-based decision-making. Professional organizations are developing results-driven clinical guidelines. Computer-assisted diagnoses, Medline searches and Internet access to medical information are increasingly in use. Best practices and benchmarking, once the exclusive property of marketers, have become common phrases in medicine. Attempts are being made to apply other business expertise and experience to medicine, especially error reduction techniques. Rigorous statistical methods have been introduced into the determination of quality.

26

Clinical scoring, especially risk-adjusted, is moving from development to diffusion phase. Both the medical profession and the public have become aware of the volume-to-outcome relationship and consequently are demanding hard data before making hard medical choices Even when results go against the accepted wisdom and political correctness, doctors are beginning to accept the evidence. [4]

...the Rest Of Healthcare Isn't.

Healthcare has three phases: 1) *Doing*, as in practicing medicine; 2) *Managing*, typified by the hospital CEO or Unit Manager; and 3) *Regulating*, for example, the Department of Health and Human Services. The *doing* phase tries to be evidence-based. You expect the doctor to have proof–analyzed prior experience–that the proposed treatment will work.

Management culture, whether in medicine, business or commerce, is not expected to be scientific. Evidence production before implementing a managerial decision is not the norm. The same is true of regulation and the legislative process.

The current *management* of healthcare harkens back to the practice of medicine in the 1890s. Consultants and management gurus sell answers "nicely packaged and marketed...that promise to solve all problems", then collect their fees and move on, just like the snake oil salesman. [5]

The Public expects the practice of medicine to be evidence-based: that is the how good decisions are made. Why does this NOT apply to the management and regulation of healthcare?

The Figure-of-8 Loop

The Figure-of-8 Loop is a solution to the problems created by lack of evidence and by "broken loops." It promotes effective evidence-based decision-making in healthcare (all elements), or at your company or even in your home. If Government adopted the Figure-of-8 loop, most of the problems we experience because of their decisions would...disappear.

A system with embedded, effective and automatic feedback would directly and immediately improve outcomes in healthcare, indeed everywhere.

The Figure-Of-8 Loop: Using Evidence and Feedback

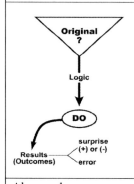

Above shows a typical linear action sequence. A question is analyzed with logic, a decision is made; results are produced–surprises and errors.

A problem provokes a test, which produces *ad hoc* evidence. The system learns from this evidence, and implements the evidence-based solution to ("DO").

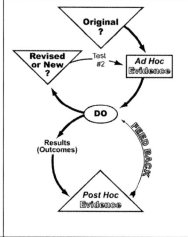

Doing produces outcomes that are measured. This produces *post hoc* evidence.

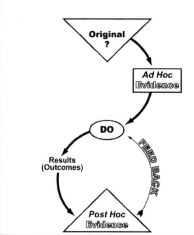

Post hoc evidence is compared to *ad hoc* evidence and the comparison is **fed back** to the doers.

A difference between *ad hoc* and *post hoc* evidence produces a new or revised question [?], generating test #2, repeating the cycle, which produces **continuous learning**.

Conclusion

We think because we have to make decisions. *Stay in [this nice warm, soft, cozy] bed, or get up and go to work? Supersize my fries or be good to my heart? What should I wear outside?* Good decisions require *evidence*–proof of outcome–and *feedback*. We cannot make good decisions about what to wear without evidence of what really is rainproof versus what claims to be rainproof. If there is no feedback to your body when the water comes through the supposedly water-resistant coat, then you will not be able to make a good decision the next time rain threatens.

Wise decision-making requires both evidence and feedback. This is as true in everyday commercial choices or family matters as it is in the health of your body or of healthcare. Without evidence and feedback, neither you nor your doctor can make good decisions. Without evidence and feedback, the manager, regulator and politician cannot make good decisions.

Without evidence and feedback and good decisions, the system does not work. We all suffer. When you ask yourself why H.R. 3590 failed to fix healthcare, one of the first answers will be the lack of evidence and feedback.

Next we show <u>how</u> a specific bad system *works* (or more precisely fails to work): the absence of evidence-and-feedback generates bad decisions, which produce perverse results, and the system fails to do what we expect or want.

Malprocess, **Not Malpractice**

A hopped-up surgeon leaves a sponge [gauze pad] inside the patient. A nurse who speaks no English mistakes one bottle of medicine for another killing a patient. Handsome lawyer in pin-striped suit drives away in a big black Mercedes after winning a twenty

> ### In this chapter:
> • Common vocabulary
> • Errors in practice
> • *Diagnosing* medical errors
> • Why have med-mal at all?

million dollar lawsuit against a greedy hospital corporation for the death of a very photogenic little girl. Do these images come to mind when you hear "medical malpractice?" They make great TV plots on *LA Law*, *ER* or *Boston Legal* but have very little to do with reality.

What do you call it when the doctor does everything right and the patient has a bad outcome? What about when the doctor does something wrong (non-standard) and the patient improves?

When it comes to medical malpractice (abbreviated med-mal), there are many widely accepted but inaccurate ideas.

Accepted Wisdom Compared To Facts

"Wisdom"		Fact
Bad doctors are the cause of bad outcomes.	**Not so.**	Bad doctors often have good [patient] outcomes and vice-versa.
Bad outcomes are avoidable.	**Not so.**	The cause of most adverse outcomes, is unknown. Without the cause, you cannot prevent them.
Patients sue providers because doctors harm patient.	**Not so.**	Most negligent doctors are not sued. Most patients do not sue.
Lawsuits help patients who are injured.	**Not so.**	Most patients who are injured during medical care get no compensation.
Legal judgments weed out bad doctors. That improves quality of our medical care.	**Not so.**	Med-mal lawsuits do not improve the general quality of medical care.
Autopsies always give us the real answer.	**Not so.**	Many med-mal suits are filed because of erroneous autopsy diagnosis.
Healthcare reform (H.R. 3590) will *reform* healthcare.	**Not so.**	H.R. 3590 exacerbates healthcare: it makes the problems worse.

Common Vocabulary

When a bicycle racer shouts, "Go ahead. Suck my wheel," he is not doing a Dirty Harry imitation. He is actually offering you help by letting you draft behind him. Words can often mean something totally different than what you think they mean.

Adverse impact refers to a patient being sicker or dead after medical or surgical treatment. The bad outcome may be due to or may be unrelated to the treatment.

Complication is an adverse impact that is definitely related to the treatment. Some are predictable but many are not. When a patient on chemotherapy for cancer loses her hair, that is a known complication of the drugs.

The Institute of Medicine defines **medical error** as "the failure of a planned action to be completed as intended or the use of a wrong plan to achieve an aim." [1] To make an error, i.e., to do wrong, what is "right" must be known. **Error** and **mistake** mean the same thing.

Malpractice = Mal [bad] + practice [from *practica* (Latin) meaning useful work] generally means improper activity or misuse. The legal definition is "Failure of a professional person…to render proper services through reprehensible ignorance or negligence or criminal intent, especially when injury or loss follows." In many jurisdictions, the phrase medical malpractice has been replaced by medical negligence.

Negligence is considered "conduct that falls below a standard established by the law for the protection of others against unreasonable risk of harm…Risk is that danger which is or should be apparent to one in the position of actor." [2]

There is a continuum of responsibility from: Unavoidable (unforeseeable) accident; to Avoidable by luck or brilliant foresight; to

Negligence, [3] in degrees from "possible" to clear to reckless, even wanton; and finally, Battery (intentional harm of defendant by plaintiff). Anyone can be negligent but only a professional can malpractice.

Risk management: Risk = exposure to the chance or injury or loss plus Management (from Italian *maneggiare* to handle) = to bring about or succeed in accomplishing; to take charge or care of. Medico-legal: "Self-protective activities—by institution or individual—seeking to minimize real or potential threats of financial loss due to accident, injury, medical malpractice, associated with the appearance of impropriety."

Tactical Practice of Medicine, also known as scorecard or defensive medicine, refers to practicing medicine more for how things look than the wellbeing of the patient.

Errors In Practice

Scenario #1: An almost disaster

In 1983, a colleague was operating on a child with a hole in the wall between the heart's filling chambers, an operation he had done hundreds of times before. I was called STAT! (*statim* is Latin for immediately) to the operating room. When I arrived, the surgeon told me that when he engaged the heart-lung machine, the child began to develop bruises all over his body. No one knew why. The surgeon finished the procedure in record time and by the time I got there, it was over: the hole in the child's heart was fixed. The child was off the pump, okay but looked like mafia enforcers had beaten him with baseball bats (bruises everywhere).

Investigation eventually found that one of the plastic connectors within the heart-lung machine had not been drilled out completely. What should have been a one-inch hole through which blood could flow easily was only about 1/64 inch wide. This caused the pressure in the boy's veins to go very high and burst many of the blood vessels in his skin. The culprit was a piece of plastic that cost less than one dollar to make.

Whom shall we blame? The surgeon is the captain of the ship. The pump technician failed to see the flaw. The medical device company made the part. The company machinist did not drill the hole properly. A lawsuit was filed against the manufacturing company because…you know why…they had the deep pocket. Had that flawed piece not been found, almost certainly the surgeon would have been blamed, sued and held negligent.

Scenario #2: Bad things happen to good people.

After open-heart surgery, it is standard care to leave a small plastic catheter with one end inside the heart and the other end outside the body. This is used to monitor the patient and typically is removed 2-3 days after operation by slow gentle pulling.

In a med-mal case after such a line with withdrawn by an experienced Physician's Assistant (PA), the child bled into the chest and died. The family sued and won, though no specific fault could be found in procedure or technique. The PA retired from healthcare.

Scenario #3: The Bristol Affair

In 1998, British newspapers chronicled a tragic story at the Bristol Royal Infirmary: needless deaths after heart surgery in children. On June 19, 1998, the British Secretary of State established a Public Inquiry Panel, what we call a Blue Ribbon Panel. Over the next two years, they took "evidence from 577 witnesses, including 238 parents…The Inquiry also received 900,000 pages of documents, including the medical records of over 1,800 children. Oral evidence of selected witnesses was taken over 96 days." [4]

The Panel found obvious and repeated medical malpractice producing a "mortality rate at Bristol [that] was roughly double that elsewhere in five out of seven years…Excess deaths, [deaths which were presumably avoidable with proper care] between 30 and 35 per year, occurred in children under 1 undergoing pediatric cardiac surgery in Bristol between 1991 and 1995."

The Panel "adopted a 'systems' approach to analysis" meaning that they would discover and deal with causes rather than simply finding a villain and blaming him or her. The Panel wrote, [This] "is an account of people who cared greatly about human suffering, and were dedicated and well-motivated. Sadly, some lacked insight and their behaviour was flawed. Many failed to communicate with each other, and [failed] to work together effectively for the interests of their patients. There was a lack of leadership, and of teamwork." *The Panel's final conclusion was that the system, not just individuals, was responsible for the deaths.*

In med-mal, people always ask: Who is to blame? That is the wrong question. Blame should be assigned to a *what*, not to a *who*.

Diagnosing Medical Errors

Is there really a problem? [5] Unfortunately, yes: deaths and complications happen that could have been avoided. Estimates of avoidable in-hospital deaths range from 48,000 to 180,000 *per year*. Contrast to ≈59, 000 lost in the entire Vietnam War or 2749 deaths on 9/11/01. Imagine the collapse of the Twin Towers *every week*, caused by a system that is supposed to protect us.

Medication errors in hospitals are estimated at 1.4 per patient, each and every time you enter the hospital. Of course, not all or even many have a serious impact but some can be fatal. Less than half of the incidents that physicians report to their insurance companies as potential lawsuits are actually filed by the injured patients. One report shows that where people are punished for all adverse outcomes,

99% of incidents (possible errors) are *not* reported. Cost of preventable adverse medical outcomes is projected at $17-29 billion per year and that estimate is more than ten years' old.

Why Do Medical Errors Happen?

The healthcare system is staggeringly complex: too many people, new drugs every day, complex machines. There are multiple, conflicting agendas: patient wellbeing; financial success; complying with regulations; as well as political pandering.

Every complex system has communication issues. Healthcare has failed to rise to the challenge. Compare the carefully choreographed communication system in a Toyota Manufacturing plant to the so-called communication *system* in any hospital.

The parts of our healthcare system were never designed to work together. Healthcare is a system that is not systematic. The parts simply grew up, in isolation. Orthopedics and Urology are grouped in the Department of Surgery purely for administrative convenience. As parts of a system, they have absolutely nothing to do with each other. Whatever organization employs the doctor is required by law to be separate from the organization where the doctor works, usually a hospital or clinic.

Complexity is made worse by the fact that others in addition to doctors *practice medicine*. Decisions by hospital managers, insurance executives, and legislators in Washington have at least as much impact on patients and their outcomes as decisions by the care providers. [6]

Toyota can predict and control exactly how the metal chassis will respond to a specific concentration of anti-rusting chemical. Every chassis will behave and respond the same way. Not so for patients. By far, the largest contributor to complexity is the unknown.

Medicine really has no one to blame but itself. It has oversold its capabilities. People now believe that healthcare can fix anything. Therefore, *if my problem isn't fixed, someone must have screwed up.*

Many people think that fiduciary means a money connection. It actually means a "person to whom property or power is entrusted [to one] for the benefit of another." That used to describe the doctor-patient relationship, but not now. The doctor has gone from near-God to fiduciary and is now approaching the unenviable position of perpetrator.

The Pendulum Has Swung.

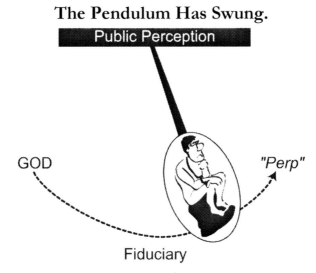

Cultural Confusion

The patient starts by having enough faith in the doctor literally to place body and soul in the physician's hands. The doctor gives medicines or operates. The patient is no better or is worse. The patient sues the doctor. Has the fiduciary doctor-patient relationship changed?

Silly question. Patient and doctor have become adversaries in the zero-sum game called med-mal: if one wins, the other must lose. The lawsuit now claims that the doctor knew better and caused the patient harm. The trust is gone and in its place is anger. Just when the patient needs the doctor most, they have become combatants.

Culturally, patient trust has turned to a search for vengeance. In the movie, *The Interpreter*, one of the main characters named Sylvia Broome played by Nicole Kidman, summarizes the feelings of a family that lost a child. "Everyone who loses someone wants revenge on someone, or on God if they cannot find someone." In med-mal, the patient can always find a "someone" to blame: the provider or the hospital.

Providers are just as culturally confused as patients. *Safety-First* has become a new watch-cry in medicine. Of course the patients should be protected, but those protections should be part of the system and not dependent on imperfect humans beings.

More important, learning requires taking chances (risk). No risks means no learning. No learning means no improvement. With the highly risk-averse culture in today's healthcare, learning and improvement are stymied.

There is a whole body of knowledge about how we humans think (cognition). Healthcare culture is plagued with muddled thinking (cognitive dissonance), [7] imperfect knowledge and bad outcomes that cannot be explained. Health care providers view bad outcomes, whether due to an error or not, as a personal failure. *Obviously I did something wrong. After all, the patient was my responsibility and suffered while under my care.*

It is a medical cultural imperative never to say *I don't know*. The doctor who is sure and certain is respected. Even when there is no clear explanation for the patient's illness or proven treatment, the doctor who wants respect and wants the patient to feel confidence, speaks with authority and certainty. In the same vein, *I made a mistake* is another taboo phrase. How can you learn to do better if you do not recognize the mistake you made (and preferably share the experience with others)?

"The most important reason [why] physicians and nurses have not developed more effective methods of dealing with human error…[is the] culture of medical practice." [8] The culture of medicine itself unconsciously accepts the Bad Apple Theory.

The Bad Apple Theory

Joan Claybrook, President of Public Citizen, a Washington, DC-based advocacy group founded by Ralph Nader, wrote the following: "The real crises are the astonishing number of medical errors and the irresponsible lack of interest among the medical profession in weeding out negligent or incompetent doctors." "Just 5% of doctors nationwide were responsible for about 55% of malpractice payouts. Just 17% of physicians [whose insurance companies] made five or more payouts were disciplined by state medical boards." [9] Her incorrect assumptions and improper interpretations worry me because you, along with many others, might agree with her.

Claybrook's diatribe is based on the Theory of Bad Apples. (A) The bad outcomes that patients experience are always due to medical errors. (B) Medical errors are due to bad doctors or nurses. (C) If we punish these bad apples or weed them out, medical errors will stop and patients will then have good outcomes. Wrong, wrong, and wrong.

(A & B) Most errors and bad outcomes are due to complexity, unknowns, and system failures. (B) All doctors and nurses make errors. They are human. Most errors do not harm patients. (C) Punishing or weeding out bad apples will actually reduce medical quality. Making healthcare more punitive will drive people away: doctor and nurse shortages will get worse, meaning more patients per provider and less time per patient. Those who remain will still make errors because they are human. Most dangerous, no one can learn in a punitive environment so medical knowledge (and therefore outcomes) cannot improve.

Who Gets Sued And Who Gets Paid?

If you accept the Bad Apple theory, you believe that doctors who get sued are the bad apples. Med-mal is likened to the criminal justice system. The police generally do not arrest innocent people, so doctors who get sued must have done something wrong. The facts say otherwise. [10]

Malpractice suits are filed primarily based on gaming the system. If there is a *perception* of wrongdoing, a suit is filed. If the lawyer believes the suit will play well to the jury, the case goes to trial. The right-or-wrong of the situation, the welfare of the victim or compensation for the family is all determined by Games theory. Also, the doctor who communicates poorly is more likely to be sued than the effective communicator, regardless of the medical outcome. Getting sued or not is determined by how things look rather than how things are.

Payouts are even worse. They bear no relationship to who needs help, who deserves compensation, or who practices high quality medicine. [11] The deep pocket gets sued. When the lawyer can create a sympathetic jury, the deep pocket pays. What happens to all those who need help but do not have a case that **appears** strong?

The only med-mal lawsuit in which I was held liable – an $8 million judgment (!) – was for the death of a child who was not even my patient. My institution was the deep pocket, so guess what happened? *Children shouldn't die* [12] *so someone must have done something wrong. Besides, they* [the big, "wealthy" University] *can afford to pay.*

Communication Is A Nightmare

Health care providers are all highly educated people. It is assumed that educated people communicate well. Effective communication is a skill just like any other, and care providers are not trained to communicate well. Just look at a hospital note or a prescription: they are unreadable. Is this what anyone would call good communication?

At Toyota plants, successful communication with feedback is built in to the system. Who communicates with whom; what information is transferred; for what purpose; feedback to whom, how and when. These are all defined in advance–they are part of the system. At an Intel Fabrication plant (making computer chips), information about every lot in process is freely available throughout the plant. At most hospitals, information about a patient is very highly restricted by law. Security concerns prevent accurate and fast communication.

The System Fails To Protect The Patient

Individuals can clearly do things to reduce errors, such as learn and practice good communication. However, to really reduce errors, we must to focus on the system, not people. In his Mannheim lecture of 2001, Tim Garson said, "We all know that individuals make mistakes but it is only systems that can help prevent them." [13]

Doctors and nurses are human and will always be imperfect. Patients must look to the system to protect them from the providers' human-ness and their lack of perfect answers.

It is actually worse than you think. Perverse and counter-intuitive results are common. [14] Solutions intended to fix problems often makes things worse. Low-tar cigarettes increase the rate of smoking. Low-flush toilets increase water usage. Screening panels to review med-mal claims actually increase the number of frivolous and unsupported lawsuits. [11]

Can You Have…?

Can you have a bad outcome without an error? You know by now the answer is yes. Healthcare people can do everything right and still patients can have bad outcomes, even die.

Can you have an error without a bad outcome? No one likes to face it, but errors occur thousands of times a day. The wrong test is done or at the wrong time or needlessly. Wrong dosage of right drug or wrong drug, without harm to the patient. Of course, the opposite can happen: right dose of right drug leading to death.

Can you have a medical error without negligence? Many people would look at you strangely if you ask this question. *Of course, a medical error is due to negligence. After all, that is what an error is.* Error means wrong and wrong means someone was negligent.

Negligence is defined as conduct that falls below what a reasonable person would do to protect another from foreseeable risk of harm. Do you think the physician's assistant in scenario #2 above was negligent? He followed standard protocol, behaved reasonably, had no way to foresee the outcome, and yet the jury found him and the Hospital "medically negligent."

Malpractice Insurance Crisis

A "subcrisis" within the ongoing crisis called healthcare is the *medical malpractice insurance* crisis. Those who deliver babies may have it the worst. Malpractice insurance premiums cost over $100,00/year for OB doctors and >$30,000/year for nurse-midwives. Their income is out of their control, based on rates set by the patient's insurance company's allowable reimbursement. Their expenses for their malpractice insurance premiums keep going up. In economic terms, supply (of dollars) is fixed but demand (for dollars) is not. Therefore, supply cannot balance with demand.

The escalation in malpractice insurance premiums is a response to the awards given and the number of lawsuits filed. Why has there been an explosion of medical malpractice lawsuits in the past thirty plus years? Were there no medical errors or bad outcomes before 1970?

In our grandfathers' time, doctors had limited ability to heal and therefore limited ability to hurt. The development of medical and surgical treatments has led not only to great cures but also to dramatic health care-induced disasters. There is a fine line between killing all the cancer cells and killing the patient. Nonetheless, we now *expect* healthcare to fix all our illnesses.

Of course there were medical mistakes and bad outcomes before 1970 but no one was keeping close track. Things are different now, especially with the transparency and volume of information available today both to the public and to lawyers.

What hasn't changed? There has been no adaptation of the med-mal system to correspond to the new realities of modern medicine. Our expectations are unreasonable. We still hold to the Bad Apple Theory. We do not ask ourselves: what do we really want med-mal to do?

Why Have Med-Mal At All?

Why have a med-mal system at all? Lost in all the tactical maneuvering, legal shenanigans, and financial calculations is what the public really wants: to help the injured and to improve everyone's health care.

Strip away the emotion and the need for vengeance. Consider objectively what we get from the present tort adversarial med-mal system and how it handles medical injuries. [15] If that is not what we want med-mal to do, what do we want?

Helping Those Injured During Health Care

Those who are injured during health care get additional care to help them recover from the injury they received, regardless of whether there was malpractice or not. I defy you to find a case where the healthcare system injured a patient and then refused further care.

The problem is paying for the additional care and, as the lawyers say, "making the person whole." Often that is not technically possible: if there is brain damage, you cannot restore the brain to normal function. The system should then compensate however it can, which translates to money.

A detailed explanation of money flow in med-mal is given in Chapter note #16. I recommend that you read it only if you have a strong stomach. The bottom line is this: the vast majority of people injured during health care get no compensation, *because the med-mal system is not set up to do this.*

Consider Workman's Compensation or No Fault Auto Insurance. In both, fault is irrelevant. All that matters is the extent of injury and what is needed to restore the person or vehicle. Contrast them to our adversarial system for med-mal, where unless you find the provider at fault, the medical victim gets nothing. Is that what you really want?

In Addition To Money, What Do We Want?

When a medical injury occurs, what do we want to happen, besides monetary compensation and a smooth recovery? We want the truth and we want the bad outcome never to happen again.

Because med-mal is strictly adversarial (win-lose), as soon as a bad outcome happens, the records are sequestered. Relations become strained, even severed, between doctor and patient. The doctors want to communicate freely and the patients need that contact. However, Risk Management takes over and follows Sun Tzu's advice to "separate the combatants." Just when we want and need the doctor-who-cares-for-me, she or he becomes unavailable.

There is some evidence that by doing the *right thing* you get the best outcome. Two hospitals, without knowing about each other, started a policy of extreme honesty. [17] Whenever a mistake was made or there was an adverse impact, the staff told the patient everything. The result was: 1) better doctor-patient as well as 2) better hospital-patient relationships and 3) fewer lawsuits. Doing the right thing might actually be cheaper.

If healthcare had learned from what happened last year to Mrs. Jones in Seattle, maybe the same thing would not have happened yesterday to Mrs. Smith in Des Moines. By far the most common reason for adverse medical outcomes is ignorance not of your doctor but of medical science. If the patients want fewer errors <u>and</u> better quality <u>and</u> less expensive care, healthcare must learn from its mistakes.

The current med-mal system discourages learning. Some would say it actively prevents learning. Since any adverse outcome might be classified as malpractice, with dire consequences to the institution and/or individual, defensive behaviors are employed. Bad outcomes are hidden or at least cloaked under legal protectionism. "Learning from error, rather than seeking someone to blame, must be the priority in order to improve safety and quality." [4] We should do the opposite of what we do now: we should *celebrate* the adverse impact, study it and learn how to prevent it in the future. The Japanese call errors "little pearls" meaning that they have value: they facilitate learning.

Dr. Lucian Leape and others describe the response of our healthcare system to a patient injured during medical care. The responsible provider is "named, blamed, and shamed" even when, as often, that person is guilty of nothing. The Bristol Report clearly identified the problem and suggested a solution: "A culture of safety crucially requires the creation of an open, free, non-punitive environment in which healthcare professionals can feel safe to report adverse events and near misses (sentinel events)… The culture of blame is a major barrier to the openness required if sentinel events are to be reported, lessons learned and safety improved. The system of clinical negligence [what we call med-mal] is part of this culture of blame. It should be abolished." [4]

So What *Should* Med-Mal Do?

While we all may have a desire to exact retribution (from someone, anyone), what we **really** want med-mal to do is:
1. Protect us so injuries are minimized (they can never be completely eliminated).
2. Help us and provide compensation when we are injured.
3. Learn continuously, so we get better and better medical care.

If you apply a systems thinking approach (next Chapter), it becomes clear that the system itself must be changed, not just parts of it. [18] An alternative system is suggested in Appendix I called The Office of Medical Injuries (OMIn). See if this will accomplish what you want. If so, urge its adoption or something like it.

A System That Thinks

Other than "healthcare," the word most frequently used in this book is <u>system</u>. It is often misconstrued in conversation when the speaker means one thing and the listener hears something totally different.

The dictionary definitions of "system" are copied below. In various ways, all of them apply to the phrase *healthcare system*. A system is:
- An assemblage or combination of things forming a complex or unitary whole.
- An ordered, comprehensive assemblage of fact, principles, doctrines, or the like in a particular field of knowledge or thought.
- An assemblage or organs or related tissues concerned with the same function.
- A method or scheme of classification
- A working combination of hardware, software and communication devices.

In order to fix our healthcare system, you need first to understand the three different kinds of *systems*: machine, complex adaptive, and what I call a "thinking system." Healthcare is a prime example of a thinking system. Each has its own nature, capabilities and limitations.

Three Types of Systems

Machine Systems

Machine systems can be physical, mechanical, chemical, even biological. They have specific parts like cogs and pulleys; or atoms of carbon, hydrogen and oxygen. The parts of machine system must be fitted together in a specific way. One oxygen atom requires two hydrogen atoms to form a stable molecule called water. You cannot combine two oxygen atoms with one hydrogen atom. Each *machine system* has defined capabilities, produces predictable results, and does not change, other than wearing out.

43

Machine systems have no free will and therefore have no purposes of their own. If we–the ones with free will–attribute a purpose to a machine system, it would be absolutely zero variability when achieving the results intended by the creator of the machine system.

Complex Adaptive Systems

Complex adaptive systems (CAS) have two attributes that machine systems do not: free will and feedback. A forest, a beehive, or a school of fish, are examples of complex adaptive systems. All complex adaptive systems are currently biologic. At present, there are no artificial intelligences as envisioned by numerous science fiction writers. "Number 5" is not alive, yet. [1]

The parts of complex adaptive systems make choices, such as ants following pheromone (smell) trails. By leaving such trails, the front ants give feedback to the ones behind saying: *this way to the food*. As a result, complex adaptive systems *organize themselves*. The parts – whether trees and termites; bees and flowers; or people in social organizations *co-evolve*.

Evolution uses random trial-and-error to improve survival. Co-evolution in people within organizations is totally different. When a person self-organizes she defines and modifies her relationship with others. Since everyone self-organizes, everyone is changing everyone else. In academic lingo, when a complex adaptive system co-evolves, it simultaneously adapts to change and contributes to change. When I talk to you, I affect you. When you talk to me, you affect me. Co-evolution means: *you change me and I change you*.

Co-evolving interactions are not predictable and therefore they produce unpredictable or what is called *emergent* results. A complex adaptive system self-organizes, co-evolves and produces emergent results for one purpose and one purpose only: survival. [2]

Thinking Systems

A thinking system has the same three attributes as a complex adaptive system–self-organization, co-evolution, and emergence–but has two additional and unique capabilities: it can direct its own learning, and it can have several intended outcomes.

A complex adaptive system uses. Over millions of years, billions of birds have used various flying formations. Those that flew in a rotating

"V" survived more than the others, lived to procreate and therefore, the wedge-shaped formations of migrating birds became the *standard* flying method. Birds–as complex adaptive systems–used a random, trial-and-error shotgun approach to solve one problem: survival.

Both flocks of birds and bicycle racing teams use the same formation–a rotating V-shaped paceline–to go fast over long distances. In contrast to the birds, the bicycle teams tested all sorts of factors such as type of bicycle; clothing and equipment; order of riders; amount of time up front. This was not a random approach. They used wind tunnels and stop-watches on different terrains and with various bicycle frames. They did something that only thinking systems (humans) can do: they planned a study program for the purpose of achieving specific desired outcomes.

Machine systems have no intentions. Complex adaptive systems have only one goal: survival. Thinking systems can also have several, different, and sometimes contradictory goals that may not even include survival. Both the 9/11 hijackers and the New York City Firefighters had purposes more important to them than living. Only thinking systems can do this and their structured learning is aimed at achieving these various goals.

Thinking systems like healthcare, with their unique attributes and therefore potential, also pose special challenges because of emergence, dis-proportionality, and multiple goals.

Steven Johnson begins his book titled *Emergence* [3] by describing how ants–"each limited to a meager vocabulary of pheromones and minimal cognitive skills—collectively engage in nuanced and improvisational problem-solving….None of the individual ants is actually 'in charge' of the overall operation…They think locally *and* act locally, but their collective action produces global behavior."

In The Wisdom of Crowds, author Surowiecki [4] writes the same thing about humans in large diverse groups. They often make very good choices and decisions. Whether the communicators are ants or humans, the results that *emerge* are not predictable.

Non-predictability may be the bane of system designers and those who demand guaranteed outcomes from healthcare but non-predictability is a *sine qua non* of emergent systems. Only thinking systems can create new things and ideas intentionally. Without thinking systems and their emergent outcomes, we would all still be huddled in caves waiting for the dinosaurs to eat us.

Disproportionate Consequences

While studying convection currents in the atmosphere, Edward Lorenz developed three relatively simple equations to explain the behavior of thermal attractors. When he combined these equations into a geometric structure, the resulting image closely resembled a butterfly's wings, [5] which ultimately produced the title of his talk: "Predictability: Does the flap of a butterfly's wings in Brazil set off a tornado in Texas?"

The Butterfly Effect was originally described as the "sensitive dependence of initial conditions" but has been extended to include disproportionate effects in either direction: small actions can have great consequences and large actions may ultimately have little impact.

Thinking systems have a special affinity for the Butterfly Effect. In other words, not only are the results not predictable but you cannot be assured of proportionality. We may spend a huge amount of money on healthcare and get little effect. We may make a minor change in management philosophy and have a massive impact.

Multiple Goals

"Individuals and more particularly organizations [thinking systems] up to governments are uniquely capable of acting *knowingly* against their own self-interest."

Real people have multiple goals that can be contradictory, even self-destructive. Patients want all the health care they think they need but, since health care is considered a right, they don't expect to pay. People who will eventually be *patients* want to eat whatever they want but do not want to have obesity-related problems: diabetes, arthritis or heart disease. Legislators want to conserve resources but still pass laws mandating services without allocating money. Doctors want to help their patients but tend to ignore resources limitations and in so doing may harm their patients.

We Need To Apply Systems Thinking

Many people ignore the broader perspective. It all seems too cumbersome. Its size is too big to grasp and impossible to change. The approach called systems thinking was created for these types of situations. It was designed to deal with processes and systems, not just the parts. When a system is a thinking one, like healthcare, the only way to help it do what we want is to use systems thinking.

Healthcare is not just a thinking system but a thinking system *squared*: it is one thinking system called Healthcare interacting with another thinking system called Patients.

As a system, healthcare is a 21st century activity handled like a 19th century assembly line. If you apply systems thinking to healthcare, its holistic nature becomes obvious. When you change one part, you change all parts. As a topical example, consider the current focus on the uninsured and what to do about it.

The Federal government plans to offer financial coverage–healthcare insurance–to those currently without insurance. Experience with systems thinking shows that whatever form this healthcare "reform" takes, it will fail to make things better. You cannot adjust financing (of healthcare) without affecting total cost, access, quality and error-rate. To fix a broken system, you must change the system *as a whole*, not one of its parts.

On the personal or individual service level (health care, two words), the lack of systems approach is both a danger to patients as well as a contributor to inefficiency and waste.

Virtually all of modern medicine is or should be provided by systems, not individuals. Your surgeon alone did not repair your heart. A surgical system did, composed of doctors, technicians, nurses, allied health personnel, administrators and support staff. (Don't forget the people who maintain the lines that bring oxygen into the OR.)

Without integrated systems, perfect results depend on perfect people and humans are not perfect. Healthcare needs systems to protect patients from their well trained, well-intended but imperfect care-givers. To optimize resource use and stop errors before they harm the patients, we need systems.

This Book Is A Root Cause Analysis

The first step when using systems thinking is problem identification: defining the signs and symptoms. We know these. We experience them every day. The second step is root cause analysis, which explains why the problem has occurred and in the case of healthcare, why it never gets better. Had the Federal government applied root cause analysis to healthcare, they would never have passed H.R. 3590.

This whole book is a root cause analysis. It helps you distinguish *problems* from *root causes*. To cure a patient, you heal/fix/dissolve the root cause. But healthcare-the-patient is a thinking system, populated by people who behave according to their cultural values. To dissolve root causes of healthcare problems, you must understand the culture of healthcare people.

People and Culture

There are six work groups in healthcare. Three provide direct care to
patients—doctors, nurses and allied
health personnel—and comprise less
than half of hospital payrolls. In the
military, these might be called foot

In this chapter:
• Work environment
• Culture and healthcare
• Three medical imperatives
• Withdrawal behaviors

soldiers, airplane pilots, and naval seamen. Three groups do not have
medical accountability: technicians, support staff, and managers. [1]
Continuing the military analogy, these would be logistics, maintenance,
and the generals.

In order to understand the people and culture of healthcare, we
need to explore concepts such as groupthink; reason versus sense; the
tarnished halo and a crisis of conscience amongst others. To fix
healthcare, you must understand health care people.

The Work Environment

Remember the wicked witch in the Wizard of Oz, who screamed,
"I'm mellllting" when Dorothy inadvertently threw water on her? Well,
doctors and nurses feel like they are drowning in new systems for
electronic medical records that are very complex and user-unfriendly.
The burden of regulatory compliance is crushing. The legal system
seems ready to pounce on anything. Instead of harnessing and
celebrating the reasons and the energy that drove people to become
nurses and doctors, the environment attacks them.

Life in the Trenches (Part A)

What are we doing wrong?! Why is everyone shooting at us?

Nurses and doctors feel like people in a bunker or in the trenches. They do not know who is shooting at them or why, or when it will stop, if ever. While down there, they keep saying: *We are doing what they want. Why are they shooting at us?* The confusion and contradictions prompts those in the trenches begin shooting at each other.

Life in the Trenches (Part B)

Why are we shooting at each other?!?

Culture and Healthcare

Fixing healthcare will involve fundamental change. Successful change requires an understanding of culture. Experts in Organizational Behavior have learned about how humans behave in groups and why. [2] Concepts such as groupthink; sensemaking; honesty; and cosmology episodes, have special relevance for health care people.

Groupthink is a behavior exhibited by members of a group where minimizing conflict is the prime objective. It is conformity made manifest. Maslow would call this satisfying our need to feel safe and to belong. [3]

By suppressing divergent views that differ with accepted wisdom, groupthink limits the options for problem solving. The logical obvious indeed *only* answer is the status quo. Envision a budget committee discussing the fact that there are too many mandated services for the resources available. A new, different, potentially better or cheaper idea would immediately be suppressed.

There is a vital difference between *reasoning*–with logic alone or with both logic and emotion–and *sensemaking*. Pure reasoning is internal: I think; I feel; I decide. There is no outside factor to position the reasoning and the decision within any context. Sensemaking requires more than good data and sound logic. It demands understanding of the situation or problem within a larger framework.

Optimizing a patient's health requires both logic and sensemaking. Using only the former, patients will not obtain the best possible long-term outcomes.

What happens when there is a difference between what an organization publicly says and what it does? What if the mission statement reads Customers always come first or Quality is job #1, but the customers wait forever and Consumer Reports says that quality is low? What do the employees think about such an organization, be it a dry cleaner, auto manufacturer, or hospital? They think that their organization's leaders are lying.

Levering and Moscovitz wrote in *The 100 Best Companies to Work For In America* that U.S. workers considered their senior managers *good* when they were honest. [4] "Honest" was defined as doing whatever managers said they would do. When there is a major difference between what the leaders say and what they actually do, the workers see the leaders as dishonest.

Every day in every hospital, people walk past a large plaque proclaiming that the patients' welfare is the most important priority. Then they go to a meeting where the budget takes precedence and where following rules is more important than a patient's comfort, even health. The result is a confused, frustrated and angry health care provider who believes management is dishonest.

A reward is a positive incentive, such as receiving money for providing a service. We pay the dry cleaner so that they will clean our clothes. We tip the waiter "to insure promptness" (tip). The hospital pays the nurse so she will care for patients. We give medals for bravery to encourage soldiers to behave bravely in combat. These are tangible rewards.

In healthcare and other helping professions, the intangible payment or psychic reward is more important than the tangible. It is not money that makes a fireman run into a burning building; or a nurse work on the trauma service; or a surgeon operate on a patient with HIV. It is the psychic reward they get.

Psychic rewards are being eroded, even withdrawn from healthcare. With downcast eyes, a colleague reluctantly admitted, "Practicing medicine started out as a calling but now it's just a paycheck." The respect once accorded nurses and doctors has been turned on its head: providers are now considered the cause of our medical woes.

Psychic rewards still exist in health care but are in danger of extinction. If the intangible rewards disappear along with the tangible, where will we find people willing to be our nurses and doctors?

People who work in healthcare do difficult, dangerous, even disgusting things primarily for the psychic rewards. What if those rewards are no longer offered? Core values and the rewards that go along with them are now being questioned.

Does the doctor really have my best interests at heart? What is more important to the hospital manager: good care or a balanced budget? Why is Risk Management using scare tactics to make the doctor behave a certain way? What should be done when there is a conflict between the patient's wishes and the provider's values? What is regulator's job: to make the provider follow the rules or make things safer for patients?

The cultural confusion has created a crisis of conscience for health care workers. They are no longer are sure of who they are. They wonder if their work has ceased to be noble and has become a job instead of a calling? Without a clear set of core values, healthcare cannot survive.

A Continuous "Cosmology Episode"

On August 5, 1949 in Mann Gulch, Montana, 18 firefighters jumped out of an airplane into a forest fire and within two hours, all but three of these experienced professionals were dead. [5] Carl Weick, a widely respected authority in organizational behavior, studied the Mann Gulch events seeking to explain how and why this *organization* literally died. [6] Healthcare can certainly be likened to firefighting. The phenomenon that Weick called a "cosmology episode" explains why the firefighters died and explains why people in healthcare are constantly confused and angry.

According to Weick, "a cosmology episode occurs when people suddenly and deeply feel that the universe [the cosmos] is no longer a rational, orderly system."

Cosmology-type events would be like the following. You watch the sun come up...out of the south! You throw a ball up into the air and...it never comes down. You do exactly what the Public asks you to do. They obstruct you, sue you, and refuse to pay you.

When the universe makes no sense, when the accepted rules do not seem to apply, when you cannot understand what is going on and know of no one who can help you: *that* is a cosmology episode. THAT is what healthcare people experience every day.

People in healthcare believe they are performing *noble work* (and they are). They do jobs the rest of the world wants. They work long, often strange hours, doing things that most people would find disgusting or just plain impossible. They agonize as follows.

If I am doing noble work, why am I being punished? If I am doing what society wants, why are they getting in my way? If they—the people in charge—want me to care for patients, why do they make it impossible to do it right?

Weick concluded with a dire warning. He wasn't writing about healthcare but could have been. In the following paragraph, I have taken Weick's clarion call and applied it to healthcare by adding medical words in square brackets.

"The recipe [*for medical disaster*] reads: Thrust people into unfamiliar roles [*nurses as managers, doctors as clerks*], leave some key roles unfilled [*not enough ICU nurses, too few translators*], make the task more ambiguous [*mandate 'all care possible or desired'…but not for illegal aliens, oh and cut your costs*], discredit the role system [*'nurses do not care; doctors are constantly making mistakes; the hospital CEO simply wants to make money'*], and make these changes in a context in which small events [*beepers that do not work*] can combine into something monstrous" [*the patient dies, needlessly*].

Their education, training, experience, and compulsive conscientiousness make providers near-perfect. Yet as many as 100,000 people die needlessly in U.S. hospitals each year. Medication errors are common. The surgeon operated on the wrong coronary artery in comedian Dana Carvey (fortunately, without fatal consequence).

Nurses and doctors make thousands of decisions every day. *Should I believe that heart rate?* (Is it real or an erroneous reading?) *What does this speck on the x-ray mean?* (Is it a tiny tumor or a defect in the x-ray film?) *Should I use the electric cautery or a stitch to stop that small bleeder?* (Which is more likely to work, has a lesser chance of damage and takes less time?) *Is Mrs. Jones telling me the whole truth or is she hiding some other symptom out of fear?* Given the number of times that care providers must "decide" every hour, it is a miracle that there are so few errors. At the core level, care providers <u>need</u> to be perfect and hold themselves to that standard. Since they cannot accept imperfection, they are obsessive compulsive in behavior and often will not (can not) see a mistake when they (inevitably) make one.

On a conscious level, the public thinks *of course nurses and doctors are human and sometimes make mistakes.* But then there is outrage when a patient suffers an adverse impact. *It must be the provider's fault. Look what happened!* Patients are just as confused and inconsistent as doctors and nurses. They can say one thing with their conscious minds but have a different expectation at the gut level.

James Champy wrote: "We have to leave behind *perfectionist* organizational thinking, with its faith in an eternal, universally right way of doing things." [7] We need both realistic expectations of individuals as well as ways that the system can protect the patients from their all-too-human healthcare providers.

Authority–Responsibility Imbalance

Providers have great responsibility and surprisingly little authority. They can operate on your heart but not order the heart valves to stock. They do not 'control' the patients but are accountable for what happens to them. This is *disconnection* in a different form, disconnecting responsibility from authority and is an ongoing sore point with doctors and nurses, like a paper cut that never heals.

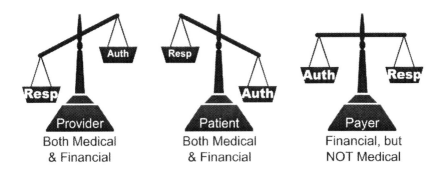

Patients too are out of balance but in the opposite direction of doctors. They have all the authority (decision making power: "Auth" in the scales in the previous Figure) but take little responsibility ("Resp") for the health consequences of their choices and actions.

Payers appear to be in balance but that too is a mirage. Payers are not supposed to "practice medicine." In theory therefore, they have neither medical responsibility nor authority. But as we all know, this is false. Financial decisions can have great direct medical impacts. Payers have an imbalance between *financial* authority and *medical* responsibility.

Three Medical Imperatives

Doctors and nurses labor under three culturally programmed and constantly reinforced commandments. Care providers are not aware that these imperatives control their behaviors. They should be and so must you, for your own good.

- Thou *shalt* make a diagnosis.
- Thou *shalt* treat.
- Thou *shalt* use the latest technology.

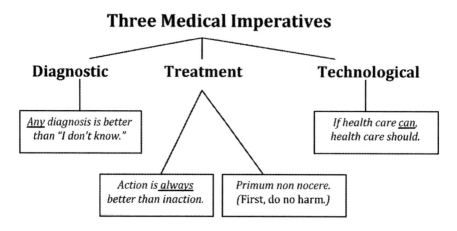

Three Medical Imperatives

Diagnostic   **Treatment**   **Technological**

> *Any* diagnosis is better
> than "I don't know."

> If health care *can*,
> health care should.

> Action is *always*
> better than inaction.

> Primum non nocere.
> *(*First, do no harm.*)*

Thou Shalt Diagnose

A doctor is not a real doctor and cannot practice medicine unless she labels you with a diagnosis. As a patient, you need a diagnosis to get in to hospital and to get out. In the hospital, you cannot get a medication without a diagnosis. After hurricane Katrina, newspapers repeatedly ran stories about people who were obviously dead but because of a back log in autopsies, death certificates were "Pending," waiting for a diagnosis. You are not a patient—alive or even dead—without a diagnosis.

A diagnosis lets people communicate more efficiently. A diagnosis allows the pharmacy computer to check if the drug ordered is appropriate for that ailment. What if the diagnosis is wrong? Hospital discharge diagnoses reported to the government are often incomplete, wrong, or manipulated for financial advantage.

There is an insidious and dangerous downside to the *diagnostic imperative*. Once the diagnosis is made, providers stop thinking. The doctor orders the appropriate medications for that condition; the nurse can go on automatic pilot; and you the patient confidently believe that the care providers understand your medical problem. After all, they made the diagnosis!

Thou Shalt Treat

The second medical commandment says that action–treatment–is always better than inaction. Unfortunately in many medical conditions, safe, effective treatment is simply not known. The treatment imperative still drives the provider to do something, anything, even if there is no good evidence. Better to look like you are doing something than look like a coward or an ignorant doctor.

Thou Shalt Treat With The Latest Technology

A woman brought a very limp duck into a veterinary surgeon. As she laid her pet on the table, the vet pulled out his stethoscope and listened to the bird's chest. After a moment or two the vet shook his head sadly and said, "I'm sorry, your duck has passed away."
The distressed woman wailed, "Are you sure?"
"Yes, I am sure. The duck is dead," replied the vet.

"How can you be so sure?" she protested. "I mean you haven't done any testing on him or anything. He might just be in a coma or something."
The vet rolled his eyes, turned around and left the room.
He returned a few minutes later with a black Labrador Retriever.

As the duck's owner looked on in amazement, the dog stood on his hind legs, put his front paws on the examination table and sniffed the duck from top to bottom. He then looked up at the vet with sad eyes and shook his head.
The vet patted the dog on the head and took it out of the room.

A few minutes later the vet returned with a cat.
The cat jumped on the table and also delicately sniffed the bird from head to foot. The cat sat back on its haunches, shook its head, meowed softly and strolled out of the room.

The vet returned to his computer, hit a few keys and produced a bill, which he handed to the woman.
The duck's owner, still in shock, took the bill.
"$250?" she cried, "$250 just to tell me my duck is dead?"
The vet shrugged, "I'm sorry. If you had just taken my word for it, the bill would have been $20, but with the Lab Report and the Cat Scan it's now $250."

The third commandment is the technological imperative: if technology *can* do something, then healthcare *should* do that something. If technology can make your skin smoother, then you should make

57

your skin smoother. If what you get isn't high tech, you aren't getting the best.

The technologic imperative is driven partly by healthcare core values but also by consumer expectations. *If the doctor did nothing more than talk to me, look in my eyes and hit my elbow with that funny rubber hammer, how does that help me? Why didn't she do a CAT Scan, PET scan, MRI, or some other high tech test? THAT is real medicine!*

In a truly <u>free</u> market, when technology improves, prices go down and quality goes up. In healthcare, improved technology generates more cost, reduces quality and increases errors. Why?

Technology Run Amok: Medical I.T.

Most doctors, nurses and managers feel like they are drowning in new, user-unfriendly information technology (I.T.) systems developed in response to the technological imperative.

Ordering, performing and evaluating a chest x-ray should be simple but is not. Ordering requires the doctor to answer a series of questions before the computer will accept the order. *Is the patient pregnant or might be pregnant?* You must answer even if the patient is male. *Have you discussed the risks, benefits and alternatives with the patient?* You must answer even if the patient is one month old. *What type and amount of contrast will be used?* Answer even if you are not using contrast.

The screen gives you more than 70 different pieces of information. Consider the time necessary to read all this and the likelihood that the doctor will miss something important when her eyes glaze over by the 20th piece of information. For "your viewing pleasure," I have reproduced what I see on my computer screen.

Data Required to Order a Chest X-ray

Name	Consent signed	Cancel reason
Alternate name	Ordering MD	Order personnel ID
MR #	Interpreting MD	Request day & time
Alternate MR#	Section	Ordered as:
Order #	Department	Allergy
Accession #	Exam day & time	Contrast agent
Status	Finance #	Contrast amount
Exam	Match	Current Rx's
Comments	Order Details	Prior study dates
Report/Results	Cancel day & time	Prior study results

You can read the x-ray *report* where you order the test, but not x-ray itself. That requires a different computer. The programs are proprietary and generally are not inter-operable between different hospitals or even for different tests within the same hospital: chest x-ray versus MRI.

Most managers in hospitals do not *manage*: they generate reports. Their work revolves around acquisition and organization of data to produce reports with titles like: Age Distribution of ER Visits by Time of Day; Efficiency of Operating Rooms; and Benchmark Analysis of Family Practice Physicians. Report generation is driven by the technological imperative. Because we *can* manipulate huge quantities of data, we *do*. Because the government requires hospitals to keep track of reams of data, they must. No thought is given to the marginal costs of data collection and report generation. Is the gain, whatever it is, worth the expense? I have no idea and, more frightening thought: *neither do the managers or the regulators.* The reports are required, the costs are huge but unknown, and you–the patients–keep footing the bill.

A Difference In Worldview

Care providers see their world as a sequence of one-at-a-time unique interactions with each patient. Standardization is for cars, not asthmatics. *Process improvement* is for hamburgers, not patients in the Emergency Department.

Managers recognize the need for standardized, efficient processes but fail to implement them. First and foremost, they meet resistance from providers. Second, managers constantly move from one crisis to another, with neither the time nor resources to design and test error-reduction methods or efficiency-augmenting approaches. Furthermore, the regulatory burden is a huge time and resource drain.

It will probably surprise both managers and providers to learn that they share core values. [8] When asked why they chose to work in healthcare, the majority wrote about responsibility to the community, altruism and the love of a challenge. Both groups want to put their capabilities to good use in the service of others.

To the extent that providers and managers relate well, the patient gets what she needs. When physicians and managers function independently (thinking in isolation; minimal interaction), the care is disjointed, less effective, inefficient, and unnecessarily costly. With providers and managers at war, it is a wonder that anyone gets decent care at all.

Withdrawal Behaviors

At lunch one day, a nurse said to me, "When my kids [her patients] do well, it feeds my soul." People choose to work in healthcare because of the moral clarity and a feeling that their work has meaning rather than just a job with a paycheck.

We could debate how to handle a suspected terrorist. There are honest and sincere differences of opinion about global warming. Should we use paper ballots or voting computers? These and a host of other important questions can be debated from different viewpoints, each side believing that their position is the moral one.

There is no debate, doubt or hesitation about the answer to this question: Is it good, right and honorable to fix a child with heart disease; to operate on someone with acute appendicitis; and to resuscitate someone in cardiac arrest? People in healthcare _know_ that they are doing good works, that what they do makes a positive difference, and that their lives have meaning.

Professional Satisfaction

Healthcare workers expect to feel good about what they do at work. Most are disappointed. Hariri reported the percent of doctors who were satisfied with their professional lives. [9]

1972 = 95%.   1993 = 65%.   2001 = 40%.   2004 = 26%.

Applications to medical schools are going down. Nursing shortages are ubiquitous. Even hospital CEOs are turning over. Part of the problem is outside healthcare, due to contradictory mandates, resource constraints and a medico-legal environment that is painfully adversarial. Part of it is internal within healthcare organizations. Most line workers in U.S. hospitals would agree with Simone's first maxim: "Institutions don't love you back." [10]

Bill Steiger, Editor of the magazine *Physician Executive*, provided worrisome data about physician morale. [11] Sixty percent were considering leaving medicine. The reasons for low morale in order of frequency were: loss of autonomy; bureaucratic red tape; patient overload; low imbursement; loss of respect; and the med-mal environment.

Steiger also asked the 1205 doctors: "As a result of working as a physician, have you experienced any of the following?" He got affirmative responses as follows: Debilitating fatigue (77%); Emotional burnout (67%); Marital/family discord (34%); and Clinical depression (32%). Suicidal thoughts (4%) are particularly frightening in physicians, who can so easily find ways to kill themselves.

Surveys taken surrounding the passage of H.R. 3590 indicate that as many as 30% of doctors now in practice will consider retiring. This would reduce access to care at a time when the need will dramatically increase due to adding tens of millions to the rolls of the insured.

The situation with health care people other than physicians is equally grim. Five-year retention of nurses is 17%. Over 80% of the nurses caring for you have been at that hospital less than five years. [12] Vacancies are everywhere and positions remain unfilled for long periods of time. Congresswoman Nancy Johnson projected that by 2010, the U.S. will need 450,000 more registered nurses and 136,000 licensed practical nurses–people we do not and will not have. [13]

Why Workers Are So Dissatisfied

The primary satisfier of healthcare providers, the reason to get up in the middle of the night, is work *content*–what they do. The primary dissatisfier is their work *environment*–the system within which they do their work. It is not about the money, and while money is not a primary satisfier, it is an important *dissatisfier*. Most physicians assumed they would eventually be assured of a comfortable living. The average pediatrician today makes less than the man who delivers baby formula. Between 1995 and 2005, while U.S. GDP increased over 40%, reimbursement from Medicare for orthopedic surgery fell 26%.

Dissatisfaction with work environment is due to the difference between what providers are *allowed* to do and what they are *expected* to do. Doctors *expect* to be able to admit to a hospital any patient who needs admission. They resent having to make what amounts to battlefield decisions about who gets care and who does not. Nurses expect to be able to spend whatever time is necessary with one patient rather than being "efficient," caring for six or eight patients. Nurses, doctors, social workers and therapists of all kinds expect to be able to talk to their patients and resent the lack of translators.

61

Doctors and nurses are culturally indoctrinated to do whatever the patient needs. When the system that is supposed to help them actually hinders them, providers become confused and angry, and look for greener pastures. When work life expectations start out so high and are so strikingly unrealized, healthcare workers withdraw.

When healthcare workers feel pushback from the system that is supposed to help them and feel attacked by the people they are trying to help, they become confused, frustrated and angry. They think about withdrawal: either turnover or turnoff.

The Turnoff

In 1973, Flowers and Hughes described the *turnoff* as the "psychologically absent." An aphorism that is currently going around warns: *We have too many people with us* [in our organization] *who are no longer with us.* Dee Hock describes "retirement on the job," and Kellerman labels such people the "isolates." [14] Turnoffs have no energy or interest beyond the minimum necessary to avoid being fired. He or she will not do anything extra at work: *if the organization is not going to take care of me, why should I go out of my way to help it?*

Turnover and Retention

Nurses and doctors are highly mobile and capable of getting jobs almost anywhere. Therefore, when professionally dissatisfied, they may leave or turnover. Repeated turnover in a workforce is called churning and healthcare is experiencing this phenomenon with bad consequences for patients: higher error rate and higher cost.

Turnover numbers are worrisome. Retention – a different and more important measurement – is terrifying. [15] In a medical center with nurse turnover of 14% per year, the 5-year net retention was 17%, meaning that 83% of the nurses hired in 2000 had left by 2005! Such low retention produces a number of undesirable outcomes: increased errors; huge costs; deteriorating morale; more vacancies and even worse retention. Low retention creates a vicious cycle. To improve healthcare outcomes, institutions must measure and then improve employee retention.

Down the Drain with Low Retention

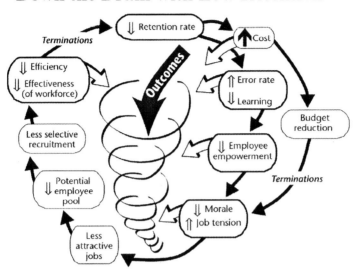

Cultural problems are rampant both within and external to healthcare. The resulting confusion is damaging to the healthcare workforce, producing tremendous dissatisfaction and withdrawal behaviors. These withdrawal behaviors hurt both healthcare workers and the patients: dissatisfied, constantly turning-over providers cannot offer optimal outcomes. After we understand why there are cultural conflicts, we can address those causes to cure rather than palliate, sedate or tolerate.

Healthcare has been described so far from a purely clinical and altruistic viewpoint without regard to money. Yet healthcare cannot exist without money. In the next chapter, we add the dollar to the healthcare equation.

The Pocket Nerve

My father-in-law was a savvy financial adviser. While claiming to know little about medicine, he said something profound about health care. *The pocket nerve is the most sensitive in the human body.*

Money totally dominates our

In this chapter:
- Money talk
- Cost/benefit analysis
- Market failure
- DX of high costs

thoughts and obscures all other issues. Before we can begin to consider what is wrong with the flow of dollars, we need to agree on what the *money words* mean.

Money Talk

Imagine that you own a dry cleaning store. You discover that it costs you more to clean cotton dresses than what you get paid. What would you do? Easy: raise the price or lower your cost, either will increase your revenue. You could then make a profit or at least stop losing money. But what if you couldn't raise the price and did not even know your cost (like most hospitals)? Answer: you either stop cleaning cotton dresses and fur coats or you will soon go out of business.

Cardiac Charges, Payments, and Costs

Diagnostic Ultrasound Test

	Charge	Payment	Actual Cost	Profit (+) / Loss (-)
Hospital	$1368	$86	$158	
Physician	$350	$85	100	
	$1992	$395	$258	+ $87

Cardiac Catheterization Test

	Charge	Payment	Actual Cost	Profit (+) / Loss (-)
Hospital	$1905	$378	$1085	
Physician	$997	$567	$400	
	$2902	$945	$1485	- $540

Costs are **true**: not allocated, estimated or projected. Payments: 2006 Medicare rates.

You sell the dry cleaning business and become the CEO of a hospital. You see the Cardiac Charges" table above, immediately call a meeting, and the exchange below takes place.

You: If we lose money on echoes, let's raise the price [he means charge] so we can at least break even.

CFO (Chief Financial Officer): You can charge whatever you like but payment is fixed [regulated]. Increasing the charge will just make us look even more high-priced than we already are. We will still keep losing money.

You: Okay, then let's stop doing things like caths and stick to things that make money.

CMO (Chief Medical Officer): No way! We cannot take care of sick patients without doing cardiac caths.

You: Well, what about just doing lots more echoes? We can make up the losses by volume profit.

Hospital Legal Counsel: Only if you want me to visit you in jail. Doing unnecessary tests solely for the profit violates several laws.

You: How can we fix this? If we do nothing, the more sick patients we have, the quicker we will go broke.

CFO: In theory, you can make money three ways. First, you can make up the losses by doing lots of profitable procedures. Second…

CMO: (Interrupting) We cannot do more tests than are medically necessary just because you want us to make money! That is unethical and as *he* (glaring) just said, it is also illegal.

CFO: (Short-tempered at the interruption) If I may be allowed to continue. You can make money three ways. You can try to get more patients with good insurance, in contrast to Medicare patients where we lose money. We can try to care for less sick patients, who need fewer caths. That would reduce our losses, but, [staring at the CMO] before you say anything, I know you won't turn patients away, so that it not going to work. Otherwise, we have to get money from the State or the Federal government. That's it. We can try to negotiate higher payment rates from the private insurance companies but that has never worked before. Besides, the government pays most of our patients' bills.

You: So, we can either try to attract paying patients just like everyone else or ask for more money from the very people who keep reducing our payments. Sounds like we are caught between a rock and a hard place. Maybe I should go back to the dry cleaning business.

Specific Money Words

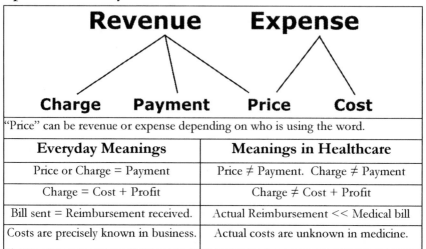

Everyday Meanings	Meanings in Healthcare
Price or Charge = Payment	Price ≠ Payment. Charge ≠ Payment
Charge = Cost + Profit	Charge ≠ Cost + Profit
Bill sent = Reimbursement received.	Actual Reimbursement << Medical bill
Costs are precisely known in business.	Actual costs are unknown in medicine.

In everyday language, a <u>bill</u> is a printed or written statement setting forth an amount of money (or charge) owed for goods supplied or services rendered. The bill is what you usually pay, but not in healthcare *newspeak* – the "language" George Orwell created in his book *1984* using common words with uncommon meanings. [1]

After we are forced by ill health to purchase sickness (not health) care, a bill is generated by a hospital, a doctor and often a manufacturer or distributor, for a drug, a device or an in-home service. Even when the charges are (rarely) itemized, we do not know what they mean and therefore cannot judge their worth. By our action of purchasing sickness care, we create a billable event, one we did not want, one we do not understand, and one that someone else–insurance company or government–will pay.

How is the bill calculated? In most businesses, the owner adds up cost and profit margin and that is the bill. In healthcare, the bill is based on a predetermined fee schedule with no relationship to cost.

In our everyday lives, we assume that the bill is what gets paid. When you pick up your dry cleaning, they hand you a bill and you pay it. *Newspeak* again: the payment in healthcare–called the allowable reimbursement–is much, much less than the bill.

Healthcare <u>payments</u> are based on fee schedules determined by third parties, such as Medicare; an insurance company; or a professional organization. Neither the hospital nor the doctor has any control over these "reimbursements."

There are no penalty clauses for late payment in healthcare. Contrast this to what happens if you fail to make your payments on your car, TV or house. (Can you say foreclosure?) Delaying payment in healthcare is highly profitable: the longer the payer holds the money acquired from insurance premiums, the more interest is accrued. Holding up just one million dollars in payments generates $5,000 profit every month for the payer–either the government or an insurance company. What possible incentive would they have to pay on time?

When you buy a carton of milk, you pay what is on the price tag. The *price* is your *cost*. The difference between how much the company *spent* and the price you paid is the company's *profit*.

In a free market business economy, the manufacturer of a product or the provider of a service determines the price based on actual (true) cost plus profit margin. In healthcare, price is called <u>charge</u>. The charge is an artificial number written down by the provider–person, institution or system–that has no relation to what was spent to provide that service or to what the payer pays. In contrast to other businesses, true cost in healthcare is unknown (see next section) and no one openly uses the phrase profit margin.

You cannot define <u>cost</u> without specifying cost *to whom* and over what time frame. For the purchaser, cost is the price to acquire. For the producer, cost is the necessary outlay of money to make a product or supply a service. A cost to the payer is provider revenue. Government reduces *cost* by reducing payments: this lowers their expenditures but increases long-term costs. It gets worse. Cost in healthcare is not calculated the way you and I do it.

When we buy a new TV, the true cost is the sum of the actual costs of the screen, computer chips, wiring, chassis, controls, installation, organizational overhead plus some profit. That is what the company charges and that is what we pay.

Ask a hospital what the cost was to provide a specific service, such as a heart catheterization or a hernia repair. They will readily quote you a number. That number is not the sum of all cost items: nursing hours; doctors' salaries; disposable supplies; amortization on capital equipment; plus profit margin. Cost is reverse-calculated: how much money did we spend last year–divide by how many services we provided and that is "cost."

This is not a nefarious collusion between hospitals and doctors. It is their response to the confusing, flatly contradictory financial system under which they are forced to function. We need to help them. We need to make words mean what they normally mean and we need to agree openly on those meanings.

"Price-Based Costing"

Before managed care, financing of healthcare was based on a "cost-plus" system. The patient's needs generated a care plan that cost a certain amount—for supplies, doctor and nurse time, hospital bed, etc. That cost—an actual cost—was adjusted for collection rate; profit margin was added (the "plus"); and the sum was the price or charge.

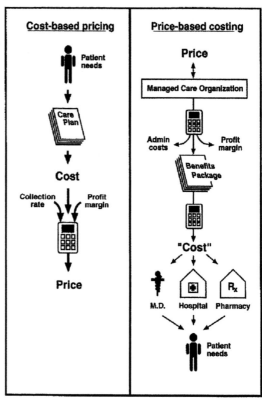

In our current world of healthcare fiscal madness, a *newspeak* "price" (no relationship to the *oldspeak* definition) is pre-determined by MediCare or your HMO. For a certain service code number, they pay so much, and for a different code there is a different payment.

Using "price-based *costing*," administrative fees and profit are first taken out of the "*price*." What remains is available for the patient. Care providers are expected to deliver all needed care using the remainder, divided in some pre-negotiated way. Note that the patient is at the bottom of this food chain. Note also that this system makes competitors out of the doctor, pharmacist and hospital for available dollars. [2]

Cost/Benefit Analysis

The Obama administration is supporting cost effectiveness research in healthcare, placed (strangely) in the economic stimulus bill (ARRA 2009). Cost effectiveness assessment is another way of saying cost/benefit analysis. Such analysis is not currently possible in healthcare for three reasons. First, there is micro-economic disconnection, which means payer and consumer are different. Therefore, "cost" to one is "benefit" to the other.

Second, true cost is unknown. You know total national expenditures on healthcare but not the true cost of individual services. Therefore, we cannot make cost comparisons, such as (a) cost of opening coronary arteries by surgery versus (b) cost of opening coronary arteries by catheter.

Worst of all, no one can determine cost *effectiveness* until health care starts measuring effects: the ones we want over the time frame in which we want them. Surrogate measures do not work and no one tracks long-term *positive outcomes*. The *benefits* that should be placed in the denominator of the cost/benefit ratio are as unknown as the true costs.

Market Failure (So-Called)

A free market balances supply and demand using money as the balancing mechanism or connector. As demand goes up, production increases to match. If demand is high and supply does not keep up or is intentionally suppressed (think oil production), the price goes up.

Is the free market working in healthcare? Most people would answer with a resounding NO! Demand for services is high and increasing. Supply is low and declining; and the price is through the roof. If you want to fix this, you must first know the *why*.

The reasons for market failure are all the disconnections previously described plus one more. Economists would say that the market does not work because it is not allowed to work. [3]

- We pay for *sickness* care but we want *health*. This disconnects reward from desired outcome.
- Healthcare measures what we spend now but not what we spend over time. This disconnects cause from effect.
- Healthcare measures only negative outcomes. This prevents us from being informed consumers.
- The patient consumes but does not pay. The payer pays but neither consumes nor evaluates the quality of what is paid for. This is classic micro-economic disconnection. [4]

To work well, a free market needs motivated sellers and informed buyers. The latter is missing in healthcare. When you buy a product, you can touch, see, (taste), and compare it. This is harder but doable with a service such as dry cleaning or legal advice. And while not strictly scientific, you can ask other people who have bought that product or used the service what they thought. Confidentiality laws prohibit a doctor from giving you names of other patients to contact.

When you buy a car, you can study Consumer Reports and compare price; miles per gallon (MPG); reliability statistics; and resale value. You understand these terms. What about dehiscence frequency; re-infection or re-stenosis rate? Consumers (patients) have much more difficulty trying to contrast results from two surgeons than Honda versus Ford.

Most important, you cannot be an informed consumer with knowing about the long-term positive outcomes you desire. In a car, you want MPG and resale value. After spine surgery, you want restored pain-free movement for the rest of your life. Healthcare only tracks negative surrogate outcomes like complications and lawsuits. They neither measure nor track over time the outcomes you want, so how can you be an informed consumer?

The "Moral Hazard"

The so-called "moral hazard" has nothing to do with morality, unless you consider spending OPM (other people's money) as immoral. The moral hazard refers to a change in behavior when one is insulated from the risky consequences of one's actions. It is like knowing you can be bad and you won't be punished. In healthcare, moral hazard refers one person's ability to spend another person's money, money that is considered "free" by the spender. You have

70

reason to carefully count the money coming out of your pocket. You pay little attention to how much is spent when it comes out of someone else's pocket. Remember **when someone else spends OPM, "other" refers to you.** All social welfare programs, not just healthcare, spend OPM.

David Goldhill wrote in the Atlantic magazine that annually the average *insured* American spends $654 out of pocket and $3,804 of OPM. [5] The average *uninsured* American spends a similar amount out of pocket ($583) but considerably less OPM: $1,103. Insured Americans consume more (healthcare services) because the entire insurance structure <u>disconnects</u> them from the market.

The market also fails because it has two agendas that are in conflict: making people well and making money. As long as these agendas remain in conflict, the market cannot achieve balance. What if people made profit <u>by making and keeping people well</u>? Then the two agendas would be aligned and the market could balance supply with demand.

A final reason for market failure is that the "free" market is not free. *Demand* is unrestrained (variable) but the *supply* (of dollars) to pay is fixed. Can you imagine a seesaw with a 1000-pound weight on only one end? Obviously, it cannot balance.

Due to this imbalance in the market, many people believe they can solve the problem with universal healthcare. Since everyone knows that countries with universal healthcare have a single payer system, everyone concludes that that single payer will fix all our financing problems. While everyone may *know* these things, it is important to consider some facts–not just bombast and wishful thinking. [6]

The USA is clearly spending more per capita on healthcare than other developed nations. The rate of *increase* in healthcare spending is greater in the United Kingdom than in the U.S. Do we still want to emulate Great Britain's single payer system?

Some tout the Canadian system as our salvation. Canada has a single payer system with publicly funded health care; reputedly universal access; a population considered responsible and self-reliant; and a small illicit drug problem. Provision of health care services consumes 43% of the total budget of the province of Quebec and is rising. [7] Still want to adopt their system?

Italy has universal health care and some of the lowest drug prices in Europe, a continent where drug prices average 60% less than the USA.

For years, the Italian government has been negotiating with drug companies, in essence creating price control of its pharmaceutical industry. Per capita, Italy also has the highest demand for drugs in Europe and some of the highest overall national healthcare allocations. [8] Between 1995 and 2003, Italy's overall healthcare expenditure rose 68% while U.S. healthcare expenses increased 40%. The Italian pharmaceutical industry, once one of the most innovative in Europe, has been decimated. Italy now depends on other countries to produce the drugs it needs and has virtually no drug research facilities. The end result of Italian government driving down consumer drug prices was: fewer drugs that work; no new drugs at all; and higher overall costs to the nation.

Take a step back. Rather than jumping directly from problem (unsupportable costs) to treatment (government control), first make a diagnosis (DX).

DX of High Healthcare Costs

In 1960, the USA spent 5.1% of GDP on healthcare. In 2007, it was over 15%. *Why* does healthcare spending keep going up, not just here but everywhere? There are ten reasons for astronomical healthcare costs. Note that many overlap, such as a action-without-evidence (#3) and reconciliation (#4) or disconnection (#5) and perverse incentives (#6).

Reason #1: New Value

The vast majority of medical conditions we can treat in 2009 were untreatable in 1960. Then, a diagnosis of cancer, leukemia, heart failure, emphysema, unusual infections, even benign brain tumors simply caused death and therefore cost nothing. Arthritis, tuberculosis, cirrhosis, and colitis all created people whose debilitation made them no longer be productive.

Modern sickness treatments (also known as "health care") are often very expensive, such as vascular stents (>$20,000 per placement); Lipitor or Coreg, each costs >$150 per month; hip replacements at >$25,000 per hip; and organ transplants (>$250,000 per organ). Coronary artery obstruction; high cholesterol; arthritis of the hip; and heart failure were much cheaper 50 years ago than today because there was no treatment possible then. Death IS the cheapest solution to medical conditions <u>as long as you ONLY calculate immediate costs</u>.

The cost number we *should* care about is **net cost estimate**, calculated as follows.

> <u>Net cost = *all* expenses - (avoided costs + productivity gains)</u>
> "All expenses" means both initial as well as on-going chronic long term costs.
> "Avoided costs" are those costs prevented in the future by spending money now.
> "Productivity gains" include productivity resulting from initial expenditures that
>   would not have been realized if money were not spent now. Failure to spend this
>   money is called "false savings" and is the way government "cuts costs."

Reason #2: More people who live longer

There are more people today than in 1900. The people alive now live longer, in part due to better technology along with general hygiene, plentiful food, and antibiotics. This partly explains the looming crisis in both Social Security financing and healthcare expenses. In 1900, 4.1% of our population was over 85 years old. By 2000, that percentage had tripled to 12.4%.

The health status of our population has powerful effects on both national losses (costs) and gains (productivity). As public health improves, largely due to improved nutrition, antibiotics, and a healthier environment, people live longer and stay healthier. Costs are avoided and people are more productive. Conversely, much of our population poisons itself with over-eating; drugs – both illicit and prescription as well as cigarettes; and an increasingly sedentary life-style. This raises costs and reduces productivity.

One estimate suggests that 27% of the growth in healthcare costs between 1987 and 2001 could be directly attributed to obesity. [9] Another report from ten years ago showed that the "cost of depression" was $44 billion per year, but only 28% was for direct care. The rest were productivity losses. [10]

Older people incur more medical costs. Annual medical spending for someone over 85 years old is 354% greater than the costs for those under 17 years of age. The fact that more people are living longer costs more money and gives new meaning to the phrase "cost of living."

Reason #3: Action without evidence

"Action without evidence" refers to making decisions and doing things without proof that the action will have the intended results. Imagine a doctor recommending a treatment without any evidence that it will help: this is called malpractice. Now imagine managers and regulators behaving the same way: this is the norm. Not only does "action without evidence" fail to produce the desired outcomes, the costs are always enormous and often subtle. [11]

When anyone acts without proof of effect, the outcome cannot produce enough benefit to justify the cost. This is true in all activities from your home to the hospital to the business world. Action without evidence translates to a negative cost/benefit ratio.

Reason #4: Bureaucracy, Inefficiency, Reconciliation and the Regulatory burden.

Inefficiency here refers to dollar inefficiency: how much money goes into the healthcare system that is not spent on patient care in any form. Virtually all estimates put this at 30-40% of total national expenditures! When you are referring to $2 trillion per year, we are into what even the late Senator Everett Dirksen called "some real money."

Though inefficiency can be attributed to "action without evidence," it should be considered separately for two reasons. How to fix it? What will fixing it do to the workforce?

Most believe that a single payer system will save money by reducing administrative costs. In 1999 in the U.S., administration accounted for 31% of all healthcare costs while in Canada with single payer, they were 16.7%. [12] Continuing this logic, we could save multibillions by adopting single payer.

Healthcare regulations generate colossal, unnecessary expenses because of the costs of regulatory compliance and because of unfunded mandates.

Both the public and the lawmakers believe (without evidence) that regulations protect patients. They give no thought to the costs. Every estimate of the cost of regulatory compliance is in hundreds of billions! Both institutions and individuals must spend the time and money to comply, with no compensation at all. Where does that money come from? Easy answer: you pay either through insurance, taxes or both.

74

The public constantly hears about the bills charged by hospitals: over $1000 per day just for a regular hospital bed and easily $5000-$10,000 per day in the ICU. It looks like hospitals are making money hand over fist. Yet, most U.S. hospitals and healthcare systems are in constant financial jeopardy. Part of the reason is how the government "cuts costs." It does so by simply reducing the [regulated] payments to MediCare and MediCaid. This may cut their outlay but it does not reduce national expenditures (what you and I call costs).

Two reasons for hospital insolvency are unfunded mandates and the resulting uncompensated ("free") care. The cost of uncompensated care in my own hospital in 2007 was $120 million, 15% of the total annual operating budget.

Contrast healthcare to other heavily regulated industries, such as airplane manufacturing or pharmaceuticals. In those industries, government regulations result in vast expenditures to test and then approve a new drug or a new airplane. The difference, however, is that the drug company or airplane manufacturer can pass on these costs to the customers by raising their prices. Hospitals and doctors cannot.

As you consider these reasons for increasing spending by healthcare presumably on health *care*, ask yourself the following question. If the hospitals, doctors, and manufacturers are getting paid less (they are); and the patients are getting less care (they certainly are): *where is all that money going?* Remember this question when considering reasons #3, 4, 8, and 9.

Just over 30% of all healthcare spending goes to people who provide care such as doctors, nurses and respiratory therapists. Another 30% goes to institutions or corporations such as hospitals, pharmaceutical companies, pacemaker and wheelchair manufacturers. That leaves 40% of all healthcare spending that does not provide *care*. This "waste of the middle" is due to the combination of excessive bureaucracy, legislated inefficiency, over-regulation and unfunded mandates. Reducing the **waste of the middle** would achieve a huge increase in cash available for care with no increase in spending at all.

Reason #5: Disconnection

In Chapter 3, we learned about micro-economic disconnection, where consumer (patient), cost-driver (doctor), and payer (private insurance or government) are all different. Such 'disconnection' makes it impossible for the market to balance demand and supply. The consumer has no reason to economize. The cost-driver has conflicting incentives: spend more for defensive medical reasons or spend less by HMO pay bonus structure. The payer has powerful reasons to economize, but the way they do it is by not paying for care.

Reason #6: Perverse incentives

If we get what we reward (next chapter), then we should reward what we want. Think about it. We want affordable, error-free health care available to all. We do not reward that.

For instance, hospital administrators can save money by cutting staff and have a powerful incentive to do so. By meeting or exceeding their budget expectations, they get a performance bonus. This incentive system produces: long waits in the ER; lying in a hospital bed until the OR is available for surgery; and not enough translators. Each is a result we do not want and degrades the quality of health care yet each is rewarded: perverse incentives. [13]

Reason #7: Defensive medicine

Defensive medicine describes actions taken by doctors, nurses and hospitals to protect themselves from a hostile legal environment. Tests are ordered that are not medically necessary but provide an objective record with which the provider can defend him or herself. Rarely does this harm the body but it always reaches into patients' pocketbooks. If providers functioned in a non-adversarial environment, one that did not consider them guilty-until-proven-innocent, they would not need to think and act defensively. Estimates of the costs of defensive medicine vary widely, from as *little* as $9 billion to as much as $208 billion per year. [14]

Reason #8: Adverse outcomes and errors

When a patient is injured during medical care or simply fails to get better, it costs all of us. The financial consequences are the same regardless of whether the adverse outcome is unavoidable or due to error. The costs include the expenses of additional care, the loss of productivity, and costs of the medical malpractice system. The Institute of Medicine has estimated that adverse medical outcomes cost the nation $17-29 billion annually. [15]

Reason #9: Money removed from healthcare

The waste of the middle refers to money that goes into healthcare but never comes out. There is a different category of cost to the system I call *money removed from healthcare*, which is money neither used for care nor consumed by the "middle."

Insurance company finances are an example. Money goes into the healthcare system as premiums paid to insurance companies: by the public for health care and by healthcare providers for liability coverage. Profits realized by the insurance companies and shareholders (probably including *your* pension plan) are by definition money not used for health care or to compensate injured patients. Whether you think this is appropriate or unconscionable, these profits represent a cost, a very large one, to healthcare.

Reason #10: Fraud, abuse, and embezzlement

It is personally embarrassing to report that healthcare has its share of thieves similar to Jeffrey Skillings and Bernie Madoff. [16] Theft, whether error, fraud, abuse, or embezzlement, generates costs in the tens of billions, including the cost-to-recover. [17]

Healthcare billing is an incomprehensible, constantly changing morass of rules and forms that vary from State to State and from agency to agency. It is not just likely but inevitable that there will be large, systematic billing mistakes that produce *unintentional* theft – inadvertent over-charging – along with the opportunities for stealing on purpose.

How do you charge for care in a teaching hospital when both a trainee and an Attending physician see the patient? What should be charged if a test is ordered that is not 'approved' for that DRG (diagnosis-related group)? Whole industries have sprung up to help health care institutions bill correctly and to maximize their income. (Their services do not come cheap,) The complexity itself has become a cost-driver and a major waste. If single payer approach is adopted in the U.S. with drastic simplification, the expected cost savings will not be realized.

H.R. 3590 and the Pocket Nerve

I must regrettably report that H.R. 3590 will not ease the pain in our pocket nerve. It is not reform (change to make things better). It is exacerbation: it fails to address any of the reasons why healthcare costs are so high.

Numbers #1 and #2 are costs we *want* to incur but H.R. 3590 assigns no new money to providers, only to the bureaucracy.

H.R. 3590 will not ameliorate #3, #5, #6, #7, and #10. They will continue to produce costs that offer no value.

The Bill may increase the costs of adverse outcomes and errors (#8) as security restrictions reduce the ability to communicate medical information and to learn.

H.R. 3590 will greatly increase the costs produced by #4 and #9.

Thus, I conclude that this Bill intended to reduce the healthcare cost spiral will only accelerate it. Do not take my word for this. Certainly do not accept the political hype. You look at each of the ten causes for high costs and ask yourself: how will H.R. 3590 affect this one? Decide for yourself.

The Final Word

We can now communicate well because we have a common healthcare vocabulary. I will understand what you mean (and you will understand me) when we discuss price, cost, or charge. As the Administration moves forward on cost effectiveness studies in healthcare, you know you must demand long-term cost/benefit analyses. Without that, the studies will be incomplete and will not satisfy you.

We now understand the reasons for high healthcare costs, separate from the media hype and political mendacity (nice word for lying). We also know what costs we want to keep and which ones we do not.

Next we turn to how to get what we want instead of being forced to accept what someone tells us we should want or have to take.

We Get What We Reward

In 1975, Stephen Kerr wrote a *must read* paper titled "On the folly of rewarding A While hoping for B." [1] It applies everywhere: at work, at home, and to healthcare.

In this chapter:
• Incentives → behavior
• Moral equivalents
• Incentives and money

Kerr described situations in which we want one thing but reward something else. We then wonder why we did not get what we want. The author describes a healthcare example in Florida. Sanity hearings required psychiatrists to determine if a person was mentally competent or not. The doctors got paid more for a finding of incompetence than for competence. Guess how many people were declared *competent!* We reward the very thing we do not want. [2]

The incomparable George Bernard Shaw decried such perversity in the *Doctor's Dilemma*, a play written when most "doctors" were charlatans and even educated physicians thought all ailments were due to infection. [3] In the preface, Shaw writes, "That any sane nation, having observed that you could provide for the supply of bread by giving bakers a pecuniary interest in baking for you, should go on to give a surgeon a pecuniary interest in cutting off your leg, is enough to make one despair of political humanity." Putting the doctor's or hospital's or insurance company's financial well being in conflict with the patient's medical well-being, puts the patient at risk.

Kerr and Shaw dramatize what is a very basic flaw: there is disconnection between what we <u>want</u> and what we <u>get</u>. Why is that? What *connector* are we missing?

Incentives Influence Behavior

If you are a parent or have parents; if you are a manager or a worker; if you have ever picked up a book on psychology or marketing, you know that incentives influence behaviors. While we all have ideals and values that affect what we do, external incentives also encourage or discourage how we behave.

If you want your child to clean up his room, provide a positive incentive like money or privileges, rather than a punishment when it is

79

not done. The effective parent or manager matches the desired outcome with an incentive that will encourage the necessary behavior.

Healthcare workers are required to function with confusing, confused and contradictory incentives. *Pay careful attention to your patient. Fill out time-consuming paperwork. Spend all the time your patient needs, but see five patients/hr. Provide perfect care. Protect medical confidentiality of but communicate with everyone who might need information on this patient.*

The Nurse is Tied Up at the Moment

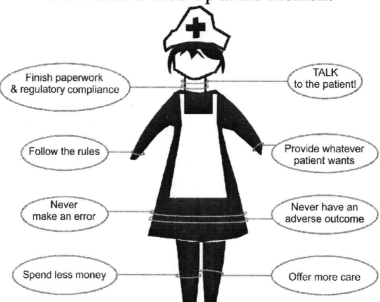

Perversity Personified

Unintended, unexpected consequences happen because we are confused about how outcomes occur. They are produced by incentive or reward systems. We may want what we want. We can expect what we think we need or even deserve. We <u>get</u> what we <u>reward</u>. That is why there are so many perverse results in medicine: we reward "A" but we expect and want "B".

The cartoon below makes health care providers laugh and cry at the same time. What about a system that rewards the service people (doctors and nurses) for bad behaviors? What incentive in today's world, other than altruism, would encourage a physician to recommend that you improve your diet, stop smoking, and exercise? If you eat-to-

80

excess, smoke cigarettes, and are a couch potato, you will need more medical care, which means doctors have more work and therefore get paid more.

Funding His Pension Plan

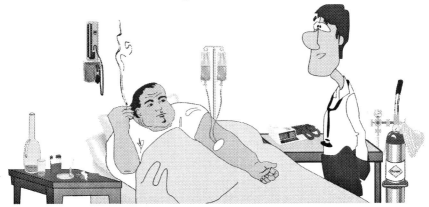

"According to the Hippocratic oath, I should advise you to give up alcohol, reduce your food intake, exercise and quit smoking. But your lifestyle is funding my retirement fund, so ..."

A new method was developed to repair torn cartilage in a joint. The operation is done through small tubes called scopes. The procedure required several small (about 1.5 inch) incisions. The operation is done using small instruments inserted through the scope without ever putting the surgeon's fingers into the joint. Recovery is quicker and less painful, and risks are reduced. The usual time in hospital is very short. Many are done as outpatient procedures.

Such minimally invasive procedures use fewer resources and therefore, payment is less for these new, better/safer/cheaper procedures than the old way. Incentives affect behavior. Which procedure will a doctor choose: the one that pays more or the one that pays less? [4]

The Market Works (Sort Of)

In the last chapter, I described market failure in healthcare. When allowed to operate properly, the market rewards actions that increase money to the public and to the government. Dollars are exchanged in a market system as a surrogate reward for what is desired: value.

The free market in healthcare does work to reward people and organizations with money. When an HMO or insurance company denies or delays care and therefore does not spend money, it is rewarded with money. When a pharmaceutical company develops a new powerful medical treatment, the company is rewarded, via patent protection, with dollars. They all compete to spend the least and get the most (dollars). In this way, the market "works."

The central problem is the use of dollars as a measure of *value*. When the competition is for money rather than health outcomes, the most dollar-efficient wins. When the *value* desired is health care service, money is a poor substitute. Indeed, when the market works well and rewards those who are most *efficient*, it is actually restraining health care service.

This confusion in market *success* is due to handling health care service as a short term cost item rather than a long term net cost/benefit calculation, as described in the previous chapter.

Volume-To-Outcome Connection

Volume has a direct and strongly positive relation to outcome. Whether you need cancer surgery, cardiac catheterization, or care for a premature baby, the more patients the institution treats, the better *and* more efficient (cheaper) the hospital becomes. [5] Health care has documented what manufacturers have known for decades: the greater an organization's experience – at building cars or violins or airplanes or providing medical care – the better you get, through learning. [6]

We need to reward the outcomes we want. We need to create incentive systems based on best available data and while we may want perfection, we should not expect it. **An expectation of perfection can lead to decision paralysis.**

Moral Equivalents

Under the old fee-for-service system before managed care, a doctor or hospital received payment for what they did. The more they did, they more they received. Clearly, there was an incentive to do more medical work leading, in theory, to unnecessary surgery or tests.

To discourage expensive and potentially dangerous unnecessary medical services, managed care was constructed with the opposite incentive. In contrast to fee-for-service, under managed care with its fixed price system, the less the provider or institution did, the more money they were paid. In theory, this prevented unneeded health care.

There were many loud pronouncements in the 1960s and 1970s about how the fee-for-service system was morally corrupt because it offered incentives to give too much health care. *My unnecessary hysterectomy or gall bladder removal paid for the doctor's Jaguar car.* The reverse is now true. *Because I did not have the surgery that I needed, the CEO of my HMO drives a new Lexus.* Rent the movie *The Rainmaker* if you want to see managed care in its worse form.

Continuing the citation of recent worthy movies, have you seen *As Good As It Gets?* A scene in that movie has become part of the urban lexicon of medical phrases. The heroine is talking to a physician about the poor care her asthmatic child has received from her HMO. He asks her if the child has had allergy testing. She responds, "No, the HMO did not approve the expenditure." He sighs with resignation and these immortal lines follow.

Carol (fiercely, to her mother): "HMO bastard pieces of shit!
Carol turns to the doctor and apologizes saying, "Oh. I'm sorry."
Physician: "That's okay. I think that is their technical name."

Since HMOs make money by *not giving* care, they do not give some necessary care. When incentive systems reward *giving* care, then we get lots of care, some of it unnecessary. Whether they use the old, fee-for-service method or the new, fixed-price (HMO) approach, *incentives affect behavior.*

With regard to H.R. 3590, there was no significant change in the incentive structures. Therefore one would not expect any changes in behaviors by patients, providers or payers.

Incentives and Money

From 1960 to 2001, the amount we spent on healthcare *as a nation* rose from 5% to over 14%. (In 2010, it will be over 17%.) At the same time, the percent of our *personal income* that we spend on our own medical care fell from 49% to 14%. We used to pay half of all medical expenses out of pocket. Now, we pay less than 15%. This

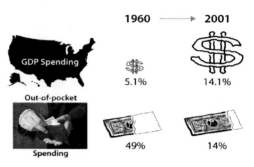

Spending Health Care Dollars

means that the individual consumer/patient has less and less *skin-in-the-game,* and therefore less and less personal incentive to economize.

Let's Play A Game Of *What If?*

At present, we reward outcomes we do not want and are surprised when we don't get what we want. To get what we want, we must:

A. Be sure of what we want;
B. Decide which behaviors will produce those outcomes; and
C. Reward those behaviors.

Simple? Actually it is. Quick and easy? Certainly not.

Suppose that we want is–(A) above–to see the doctor quickly. The behavior–(B) above–we want is an appointment in the next 2-3 days. Finally, suppose the actual *cost* for the doctor and her office for is $150.

What would happen if the system *rewarded*–(C) above–the doctor as follows: $250 for an appointment within 72 hours; $200 if within a week; $150 if appointment within two weeks; $100 if appointment occurs later? What would happen? Answer: Doctors and clinics would find a way to dramatically reduce waiting times. It's that simple.

We get what we reward. We reward what we measure. To get what we want, we must measure the things we want. Healthcare does not measure those outcomes. In healthcare, the measuring cup is upside down.

Cupside Down

- ☐ Imagine a school that only kept track of students who flunked out.
- ☐ Would you buy a car from a company with sales brochures showing the ones that exploded?
- ☐ Would you invest in a corporation that measured only customer complaints and that stocked only those products that did not sell?
- ☐ What about a human resources department that kept track solely of those people who left the company (turnover), but not how long people stayed? [This describes most companies.]
- ☐ Would you go to a hospital that only knew how many patients died, had complications or sued them? [You already do.]

Good Decisions Need Good Measurements

Every waking moment we make decisions. Should I wash my face or brush my teeth first? What should I wear? Can I make it through that yellow light? Every decision requires a measurement. Measurements are decision aids. They help us make better decisions.

In this chapter:
• Good decisions need…
• *What* is measured?
• *How* do they measure?

Russ Ackoff wrote, **"knowledge** is conveyed by instructions, answers to how-to questions [while] **understanding** is conveyed by explanations, answers to why questions. Information, knowledge and understanding enable us to increase efficiency, not effectiveness. [1]

Efficient and not effective?

You can be efficient and not be effective. If you drive an aerodynamically designed hydrogen car at the optimal speed over the smoothest roads, you can be very fuel-efficient but if you drive in the wrong direction, you will not be effective in reaching your destination. To be effective requires wisdom (good judgment).

"Understanding" involves an answer to the <u>why</u> question. **Wisdom** requires the exercise of judgment between competing <u>*why's*</u>. Wisdom is making a choice among relative values. Thus, it requires wisdom to decide between the following alternatives–*each* is a good choice.

Should I?   • Spend fewer tax dollars.
            • Treat people with diabetes.
            • Prevent potential complications of diabetes, in the future.
            • Fund research to find a cure for diabetes.
            • Spend more on diabetes than on cancer.

Effectiveness is the result of wise choices. While it should include efficient use of resources, effective decisions involve evaluating alternatives, possibly innovating new ones, and balancing all factors to achieve the best result possible. Peter Drucker made this succinct, helpful operational distinction: "Efficiency is doing things right. Effectiveness is doing the right things."

Being Effective In Healthcare

The difference between **efficiency** and **effectiveness** is critical in healthcare both as patient and as provider. Efficiency deals with use of resources: money, people, information, and physical objects such as cement or steel girders. **Effective** means you get the effects you want and avoid the ones you don't.

Always ask: we need to be efficient to achieve what *effect*?

In healthcare, there are no shareholders but billions of stakeholders. The answer to the question "efficiency in the service of what?" should be: efficiency in the service of this effect: a healthy, long-living populace. In this context, do you want an "efficient" doctor, one who sees 30 patients in an hour? In this context, would you go to a hospital where nurses are "efficient" meaning they handle 10 or more patients per shift? [You probably do.]

As the administration in Washington pushes cost effectiveness studies in health care, we need to be very clear about what "effects" we want. In healthcare, efficiency and effectiveness can be opposites!

Why Do We Need To Decide *Anything*?

You make decisions because you have a problem. You decide in order to solve your problem. When you purchase a car, you are acquiring a solution to the slow and uncomfortable travel method called walking. If the distance is long even for a car, you might decide to purchase an airplane ticket. When you decide to buy a hamburger at McDonald's, you are solving (temporarily) a problem called hunger.

When you go to a lawyer for a will or a pre-nuptial agreement, you have decided to solve a potential future problem in advance: what to do when you die or if your marriage does.

In his book *The Agenda* [2], Hammer relates a "story about an annual meeting of a manufacturer of power tools. The chairman stands up to address the assembled share- holders and say, 'I have some bad news for you.' 'Nobody wants our drills.' The audience was shocked. At last report, his company

> ### **ALWAYS keep in mind:**
>
> We do not buy products.
> We do not buy services.
>
> We buy answers.
> We buy solutions.

had a 90 percent share of the drill market. He went on, 'That's right, nobody wants our drills. What they want is holes.'"

We make decisions in order to solve problems. To make good decisions, we must have good data, which starts with proper measurements.

What Do They Measure?

Current Measure	Preferred Outcome
Cost (short-term)	Long-term productivity
Error rate	Better health
Adverse impact	Better function
Complication	Intended (**+**) effect
Mortality	Long life
Turnover of workers	Retention of workers

- **They measure what we do not want rather than what we do want**. They measure number of people who die or have complications; errors and adverse impacts; the dollars spent in the present fiscal cycle; incident reports; and lawsuits.
- **They measure what is easy to measure rather than what we want**. They keep track of deaths, complications, recalls, turnover, length of hospital stay, and immediate cost.
- **They measure the now and ignore the later**. They worry about this month's budget and annual turnover with no regard to: net 5-year retention; improving personal productivity as well as longevity; and reduced long-term costs.

- **They measure too much because it is easy to keep track on computers.** Every hospital keeps track of the number of people who enter the ER by time of day, ethnicity, age, gender, payer status, time till seen, time in Radiology, time in ER, diagnostic codes, procedures done, drugs administered, cubicle number, and so on. "If we were to set out to design an efficient system for the methodical destruction of our community, we could do no better than our present efforts to…reduce life to the tyranny of measurement." [3]
- **They use inappropriate surrogate measures.** We measure a 2% mortality rate and assume a 98% survival rate as though they are simple opposites like black and white. Death has no gradations. Life docs: one can be fully functional, or be paraplegic, have urinary incontinence, or be unable to bear children. Using the inverse of death (a bad outcome) as the measure of life (the good outcome) is an inappropriate surrogate measure.
- **They measure process/intermediate results rather than final outcomes.** They keep track of time-in-hospital, 30-day survival after surgery, and turnover of nurses. The first is a process metric, the second defines a "surgical success" even if the patient dies on day 31. They want nurses to stay on the job but we only measure how often they leave.

We *Get* What They Measure

This business adage has been proven over and over: *what gets measured gets better.* **We _get_ what healthcare measures**. This is true in building cars, growing vegetables, or brain surgery.

Your organization tells you what is important by what it measures. You pay attention to what your boss thinks is important. Because you focus on what is measured, that activity improves.

What is measured – and therefore is important – to healthcare?

        ☐ Cost
        ☐ Deaths, Complications & Bad Outcomes
        ☐ Compliance with regulations
        ☐ Lawsuits
        ☐ Length of hospital stay

Healthcare does not measure restored productivity of the patient; improved function of the patient; or longevity of the patient. Is it any wonder that we do not get restored productivity, improved function, or longevity?

We *get* the outcomes. To see if we get what we want, healthcare needs to measure all outcomes, but especially those we want: positive long-term outcomes. Outcomes can be intended or unintended, beneficial or adverse. [4] There are variations to keep in mind.

- o A patient can have an adverse impact that was no one's fault.
- o A complication need not be adverse but often is.
- o Errors are common in medicine, many without any impact.
- o Most adverse impacts and complications are not due to mistakes.
- o Unintended consequences can often be adverse, occasionally advantageous, and always provide the potential to learn.

Quality *Assurance* – A New Oxymoron

Every hospital has a quality assurance (QA) office that, in theory, is supposed to assure high quality patient care. They do nothing of the sort. If QA tried to assure quality, they would have to define quality, then measure it, and finally take a proactive approach to improve it. That is not what they do. "Regardless of quality initiatives, health care systems undertake little comparable quality measurement." [5]

Most QA offices track outcomes that have already happened and compare them to benchmark standards. "Quality" is not defined. If the QA office of a Hospital finds that they are doing above average, they conclude that their hospital is "assuring quality."

QA measures compliance with guidelines. They track whether nurses and doctors follow rules and regulations – yes or no. Only negative medical outcomes are measured: adverse impacts, errors and lawsuits. There are no positive measures, no indicators of good quality.

The current system strongly discourages risk-taking and supports the status quo. If healthcare is provided strictly by the rules, then they have *assured quality*. If someone has an idea to reduce the current 10-hour wait in the ER or two days in hospital for a heart catheterization or five days in hospital after delivering a baby, the system discourages testing the new way. It says that deviation from the norm is, by definition, poor quality.

Quality Assurance is a misnomer: it assures stability and compliance, not quality.

How Do They Measure?

Light travels at 299, 792, 458 meters per second. The melting point of copper is 1357.6 Kelvin. In many disciplines, a precise answer is known. Every time you combine H_2O with CO_2, you get H_2CO_3–same result every time, without fail. In many disciplines, you can predict individual results. Healthcare is not one of those disciplines.

The current level of medical knowledge is primitive compared to the natural and physical sciences. Astronomers can predict with assurance exactly where Jupiter will be in 423 years and nine days. Physicists know absolutely that every time critical mass is achieved, there will be a nuclear explosion. But ten milligrams of lasix–a drug that makes you urinate–can have very different effects in ten people even of similar size. Doctors do not know why. Treatment for childhood leukemia works in eight out of ten children. Why not the other two? Doctors do not know why.

Providers of health care cannot make an accurate prediction to any one patient. They can offer probabilities but not guarantees. Therefore, healthcare must resort to statistics and benchmark surveys.

Statistical Probabilities

If you cannot predict a specific outcome for a specific individual, you can lump patients into large groups so that statistics can be applied. The larger the number of samples–bottles of shampoo; cars that get >30mpg; people with rheumatoid arthritis–the more "robust" will be the statistical calculations. Robust means more accurate predictions but only for statistical populations. No matter how accurate you get in predicting for populations, you still cannot predict for a single person.

Suppose a person has a pulmonary embolus (blood clot blocking flow through the lungs) and no specific cause is found. (This is very common.) Doctors will tell that person that there is a 20% chance that it will happen again. Now give the person who had the embolus a name and address: Mrs. Ethel Jones of Manhasset, NY. Mrs. Jones does not have a 20% risk of recurrence. She has 100% or zero. For her, it either will happen again (100% chance–a sure thing or it won't (zero probability–another sure thing). Statistics apply to groups, not individuals.

Benchmarking

A benchmark survey is a market survey with fancy statistics. Typically, a private company is hired to survey a group of people–those who bought a Kia or people entered an ER–to determine what happened and how they felt about it. Responses are compared to other groups of people – those who bought a Honda or those who went to an ER at a different hospital.

The biggest problem in benchmarking is that most people do not respond. Response rates of 18-24% are considered very high. The usual response rate is 3-5%. The only people who respond are those who feel very strongly and are willing to spend the time to answer. This is selection bias, and you do not know which way the bias leans: positive or negative, for or against. How much can you depend on a survey where 76% to 97% (!) of the people do not answer?

The latest healthcare survey fad–Benchmarking Best Medical Practices–tends to encourage mediocrity. As long as you are doing better than most, you have a "Best Practice." This is the opposite of what highly successful companies say: "Good enough never is." [6]

Surveys can actually be harmful, particularly internal satisfaction surveys of a healthcare workforce. When an employee is surveyed three times in five years and nothing changes, the message from administration is clear: *whatever you say on the survey, we are not going to listen.*

Relative Measures Versus Absolute Measures

The problem with benchmarking in healthcare is easy to understand when you answer this question: What is the hospital trying to achieve? If it is the best among one hundred institutions and has a mortality rate of 10% after heart surgery, that is *not* what patients want. Patients want zero mortality and do not care whether a hospital is number one or number fifty. Competitive position is important only *after* you have achieved the minimum acceptable standard. In other words, the absolute measure is most important and the relative measure is next. Either alone will not suffice. *You need both.*

Suppose you are driving your car toward a four-way stop. Approaching the intersection on your left and quite close to you is a bicycle rider who might hit you. On your right, further away from you is a big truck that also might crash into your car. Which one should

91

you worry about: the nearer or the more dangerous? The answer is both. Just as you need to consider both the immediate and the more dangerous threats, so you need both relative and absolute metrics.

To appreciate fully the results of *any* process from open-heart surgery to open-hearth cooking, you need **BOTH** <u>absolute</u> **and** <u>relative</u> **positive,** <u>direct</u> (non-surrogate) **outcome measures**.

Surrogates Lead Us Astray

A surrogate measure is a substitute for what you really want to measure. When you look at your thermometer outside your window, you are using the number as a surrogate for the air temperature. What you really want is the weather report so you can decide what to wear. The price of a stock on the NASDAQ is a surrogate for what the market thinks the company is worth, which in turn is a prediction of future earnings.

Surrogate measures can be positive or negative, <u>*not*</u> meaning good or bad. A positive surrogate moves in the same direction as the measure of interest: when the stock price rises, your wealth goes up.

Negatives ≠ Opposites of Positives		
Negative		**Positive**
Absence of pain	≠	Pleasure
Reduced cost	≠	More money
Error-free Medicine	≠	Good health
Following regulations	≠	Good health
Not being sued	≠	Having good result

A negative surrogate moves in the opposite direction from the measure of interest, like a seesaw. Almost all the measures in healthcare are negative surrogates: cost, length of hospital stay, errors and surgical mortality: as they increase, we get less of what we *want*.

Healthcare uses absence of a negative to infer a positive. Not being dead = being alive, but there are gradations of being alive. Absence of pain is not the same as having pleasure.

Regulations Are Surrogate Measures.

At variable times but typically every five years, the Joint Commission on Accreditation of Healthcare Organizations (recently renamed The Joint Commission) inspects every accredited hospital in the US, over 5000 of them. The Commission has established a wide array of rules and regulations, such as: Doorstops are forbidden. There is a specific approved number of electrical outlets in a nursing station, etc. The inspectors determine if the hospital is following regulations. If not, the institution can be warned, cited, even closed.

The stated purpose of an inspection is to protect the patients from dangerous practices and procedures. The reasoning goes that the regulations describe good practices and that following them assures good outcomes. Regulations are surrogates for medical outcomes.

As a surrogate for good medical outcomes, regulations are a bust. They punish and never reward. Following regulations formalizes behaviors that have no relation to outcomes that patients receive. For instance, JCAHO now demands that "mcg" is the only proper abbreviation for micrograms and "μg" is unacceptable. They claim that the latter is more likely to be misread without any evidence this is so or even that a problem exists.

Regulations increase cost and complexity, demanding more tracking and more reconciliation, producing even more regulations and more cost. Regulations create positive feedback loops that encourage the very things we do not want. **Regulations are** *really bad* **surrogates.**

Measuring Wrong Prevents Deciding Right

In healthcare, they measure "wrong," use surrogates, and, do not measure for long enough. Healthcare suffers from tunnel vision and the tunnel is much too short: the time horizon for outcomes' measurement is next month's budget when it should be our lifetimes.

For a baby with a congenital heart problem, the time horizon for success is 100 years of healthy life, not 30-day survival after surgery. The therapeutic relationship does not end until life is over. The outcomes we want from healthcare are decades in the future.

Preventative care keeps people healthy. It is cost effective both because it improves national productivity and because it costs less in the long run. It is always cheaper to prevent acute asthmatic attacks or complications of diabetes than to treat them. *The last sentence is true only when you count your costs over the long run.*

If we measure right, are willing to learn, use systems thinking, and are culturally sensitive, then we are ready to practice good medicine – on healthcare.

Practicing Good Medicine

Imagine that you are a doctor walking down the street. You come upon a woman lying on the sidewalk. Surrounding her are four people all talking at the same time. One person is offering a candy bar while another is selling

his unique, patented, guaranteed, for today only just $19.95 plus tax but only if you act now! A third is giving CPR and the fourth is threatening her with a charge of public drunkenness.

What should you do?

Observing this scene reminiscent of the *Three Stooges*, you ask, "What is wrong with this woman?" They all start speaking at once, suggesting diabetes, low self-esteem, a heart attack, and vagrancy. No one has examined the woman or even tried to talk to her. You shake your head in amazement wondering how anyone could possibly try to treat much less cure a patient without first knowing the diagnosis–the cause of her illness.

The woman lying on the sidewalk is Healthcare. The doctors-without-licenses are legislators, insurance executives, expert consultants, and regulators. YOU are the doctor, or will be after finishing this book. The book is a do-it-yourself treatment guide. What should you do?

The cynic or turn-off would walk away mumbling that the woman is terminal and is going to die anyway. This self-styled realist has created a self-fulfilling prophecy. <u>Only when we pre-accept defeat will defeat be sure</u>. When President Kennedy said we would put a man on the moon – *when* he said it – it *was* impossible. Nine years later, we did it. You, me, all of us have to start with one agreement, one commitment: **healthcare must be cured and we can do it.**

Healthcare is a critically ill patient who needs to be fixed, meaning cured. The following people *cannot* fix healthcare: Washington, State governments, AMA, advocacy groups, Unions, big business, big insurance, big pharma, trial lawyers association, unions. These are all major stakeholders in healthcare *as is*. Each has a personal agenda that often conflicts with what you and I want from healthcare. They cannot fix it. Only you can. *You* need to become the doctor for healthcare.

As the doctor, you want to practice good medicine. This starts with taking a history, doing a physical exam and reviewing evidence–both in the medical literature and tests on this specific patient. All this leads to the first level: making the diagnosis of why the patient is sick.

People say over and over that the system is broken. The truth is, healthcare developed without any plan, system or roots. It is called a system but it is not. It is like a tree without roots. Imagine the tree on the front cover with no roots. How long could it stand?

The greatest strength of our nation is its roots, which are the principles on which the USA was founded. It is these principles that guide us through difficult times and advise us when decisions must be made. We may argue about the interpretations of the principles but no one questions that we have common roots or principles.

Healthcare has no agreed-upon roots or principles. The roots under our present healthcare tree developed separately and in competition. They steal water from each other and nourish themselves but not the tree. There is no system of roots that helps the tree flourish.

To fix healthcare, we need *system* where we now have *chaos* (no system). Our tree needs good roots – principles that we all accept. No group other than the Public can or will do this. WE are the only ones who can fix healthcare. Fixing starts with the root causes of healthcare *sickness*. That is what the first half of this book does: it turns the reader into a diagnostician for healthcare.

Understanding Leads to Answers

Once you understand the root cause of a problem, the solution generally becomes clear. Henry David Thoreau wrote that, "All perception of truth is the detection of an analogy." An analogy of healthcare with the two-master dilemma improves our understanding.

The two-master dilemma was recently dramatized in the news business in the movie *Good Night and Good Luck*, about the fall of Edward R. Morrow. Morrow believed that the newsman's first and highest calling was to report the truth. [1] The CEO of CBS, Leslie Moonves said that reporters must offer "better stories told by attractive personalities in exciting ways" in order to be entertaining. [2] The two-master dilemma is summarized by a three-word question: which comes first – reporting the news or entertaining the audience?

A medical insurance company also has two masters: public and profit. The public master, called the client or patient, demands that the insurance company pay for all healthcare services, regardless of cost. The profit master, collectively called shareholders, demands that the company make money and therefore *not* pay for health care services.

The two-master dilemma is the best explanation of the bizarre behavior of the CBO (Congressional Budget Office) in 2010. In January, the CBO estimated that the healthcare Bill would <u>add</u> $1 trillion to the national deficit. In March, the CBO announced that the same Bill would <u>reduce</u> the deficit by the same amount. In January, the CBO was apparently working for its *public* master and in March, it was working for its *pay* master (the Federal Government).

The two-master dilemma is everywhere, including your welfare versus your employer's or even your spouse's. Superficially, it seems insoluble: some one has to come second. However, if you look deeper at the root of the dilemma, the problem is not the existence of two masters but the fact that they are in a win-lose scenario—an either/or choice. As long as it is *either* I do well *or* my company does well, then the problem truly is insoluble. But what if you changed the game to a win-win arrangement?

What if you did well when your employer did well? What if reporting the truth actually was entertaining? What if the patient's health coincided with the insurance company's financial health? Suddenly, the two-master dilemma ceases to be a dilemma.

Healthcare Is Making Us Sick

Healthcare is making us sick on two levels: individual and national. We are all well aware of the first. Most people have limited understanding of the second.

Newspapers regale us daily with medical disasters, mistakes and suffering patients. Safety is a watch cry but not a reality. Regardless of whether the error was avoidable, when there is a bad healthcare outcome, a person with a name, a family and a mortgage–a specific human–suffers. When people do not get regular checkups because of lack of health insurance, and wait until a condition becomes a crisis, medical outcomes are worse and costs rise. Access limitations to healthcare can make us sick, as individuals.

The headlines constantly talk about more than *47 million people without insurance*. Between 1989 and 2005, the number of people without health insurance rose from 31 million to 44.8 million. This represented almost a 50% increase in the total number of uninsured and a 2.5% increase in the percent of the U.S. population without health insurance. The problem is getting worse both absolutely and relatively.

Healthcare is also making us sick *as a nation*. Notice the headlines about outsourcing and jobs going overseas? Craig Barrett, Chairman of Intel warned: "Every job that can be moved out of the United states will be moved out…because of health care costs. The health care system is out of control. It's unstable; it's basically bankrupt. It gets worse each year and all we do is tinker around the edges when what we need are major fixes." On the very same day in 2006 as Barrett's speech, the Kaiser Family Foundation, a healthcare think tank, reported that healthcare premiums rose 7.7% the prior year. This was almost double the rate of inflation.

American automakers will say that the most expensive component of a US-made car is not the chassis or computer components but the health costs of their workers. Same thing for Boeing and airplanes except that liability premiums are number one and health costs are number two. Healthcare is sapping our national strength.

The Nature Of Healthcare

Healthcare includes people called providers at their very best caring for other people, called patients, who are temporarily at their very worst. Both are imperfect–they are human. Providers never choose to make a mistake. Patients do not choose to be sick. No one wants to go to the doctor or to the hospital. Healthcare provides a service that we would rather not use, but must.

Results in health care are due to interactions of many people: doctors and nurses; allied health personnel; pharmaceutical and device manufacturers; managers; insurance people; as well as regulators and legislators. Health care is not a solo sport. "The days of the one-ill, one-pill, one-bill doctor are over." [3] That is even truer today than 35 years ago when it was written.

A computer industry friend joked: *Faster; Cheaper; Reliable. Pick two.* Healthcare people quip*: Better; Safer; Compassionate; Cheaper. Pick one…maybe.* These adages reflect the zero-sum game: If you win, I lose. If it is better, it must cost more.

In their bestselling book *Built to Last*, Collins and Porras wrote that great companies reject the "either/or"–the zero-sum game–and demand that their employees use the "genius-of-the-And." With this attitude, an Apple designer would say *I want our new computer to be faster,* and *more reliable,* and *to cost less.* The hospital CEO would challenge his senior planners to reduce cost while improving service and producing better long-term results. In the 1980s, we proved that you could have both better and cheaper in health care at the same time. [4]

Doctors and nurses understand that health care is more art than science. Most of what they do trying to heal sick people is guesswork, based on limited information. There is no testing possible in medicine like what is done in a chemistry lab or Tesla Motor Company.

When authors write about the indeterminate nature of healthcare, they should give credit to the brilliant German physicist Werner Heisenberg of rocketry fame. He elucidated a fundamental truth, as applicable to healthcare as to physics.

The Heisenberg Uncertainty Principle states that, "The more precisely the position [of an electron] is determined, the less precisely the momentum is known." Translation: absolutely *perfect* knowledge and therefore *perfect* predictions are impossible. Prediction becomes a matter of statistics and probability, not some certainty guaranteed by enough information and meticulous measurements.

You cannot reason your way out of the Uncertainty Principle. You cannot drown it in a sea of data, though that is precisely what we try to do. We gather more and more data using modern computer capabilities because we *can*. We study longer and harder. We apply more and more logic to solve our problems. We hire consultants because one of them *must* have the answer. When the answer is not forthcoming, we blame the doctor or the consultant or the data. We never name the real culprit: the indeterminate nature of healthcare and the impossibility of sure prediction. The patient sees medical science just like physics or mathematics. Therefore, *there is an answer for every problem. Just like those who have mastered physics or mathematics, the good doctor knows the right answer.* Mathematicians know the specific answer to a complex equation. The statistical probability that 2 X 2 X 2 = 8 is 100%–certainty.

For the good doctor, there are no patient certainties. The good doctor knows that drug X works in 85% of people, doesn't work in 10% and makes 5% of all the people who take it feel worse. What she does not know is whether you are one of the 85%, the 10% or the 5%.

People say that everything is in the genes. They are right but few really understand what that means. Your genome–your unique genetic code–is not just the blueprints to build your body, but also the instruction manual for how your body works. When you take a medication, your genes tell your liver what proteins (chemical tools) to make. These proteins will alter the chemicals in the drug: convert them into several new chemicals that have effects in your body. The liver then makes more new proteins (again under genetic instruction) to break down the chemicals and get rid of them (out of your body, usually in the urine.)

Pharmacogenics is a new medical field that studies how the genes in our cells interact with drugs we take. Pharmacogenics holds great promise for turning medical probabilities into individual certainties.

We all have different genomes–different instruction manuals. Therefore, two patients with two different genetic codes will handle the same drug differently. In the 85/10/5 drug example (above), the genome in 85% of people makes proteins that change the drug into a helpful chemical. In 10%, the genes change the drug but without beneficial effect, and in 5 out of 100, the drug is converted into something that hurts the patient. At present, no one can identify which group you are in.

When pharmacogenics realizes its promise, your doctor can analyze your unique genetic code and know, absolutely, what the drug will do to you; what side effects you personally will experience; and which medicines to avoid. When pharmacogenics fulfills its potential, there will be guarantees. Until then, there are none.

Is there another activity on earth where you ask someone to cut you open and then thank them afterward? Who else do we pay for the privilege of listening to our deepest, scariest, most intimate thoughts?

The only thing that comes close to the deeply personal relationship of doctor and patient would be with a religious counselor.

Patients are human and so are doctors and nurses. Each brings personal genius and foibles, strengths and character flaws. Healthcare providers do things that entail risk, often life-and-death decisions. Because they are human, the providers feel intense anxiety: by their direct actions and though intending to help, they can harm, even kill, another human being.

Healthcare can offer truly unique forms of satisfaction. There is no personal gratification comparable to bringing a baby back from death. For those in critical care types of medicine, such as trauma physicians, ICU and other interventional teams, the gratification is immediate and extremely intense. (Of course, the care providers must also be emotionally open to the bad outcomes, where a patient dies under your care and you are devastated.)

The boy holding the very large pencil won his elementary school spelling bee. His brain works just fine. When he was born, he was critically ill with a congenital heart defect that allowed very little oxygen into his blood. He required a middle-of-the-night catheter procedure then open-heart surgery. After spending his first month of life in the hospital, he has been a completely normal child.

The people who cared for this child feel intense satisfaction. This includes the doctors and nurses; the cath lab, echo and OR technicians; the transport teams; and the people in central supply who found or created the wires and catheters needed.

Administrative and support people in healthcare often work very hard and receive little of the personal gratification available to providers of direct care. This is unfortunate. Healthcare managers have similar core values to doctors and nurses, such as altruism and service focus yet they often do not receive the emotional payback, the same sense of personal accomplishment.

Making The Diagnosis (DX)

There are two kinds of diagnoses: descriptive and etiologic (causal). You want the second.

Rheumatoid arthritis and fibromyalgia are descriptive diagnoses associated with chronic pain in joints and/or muscles. Healthcare treats symptoms *because no one knows the cause* (etiology).

Diabetes is an etiologic diagnosis: we understand that the sugar imbalance is due to low insulin. By regulating the insulin level, the patient is "cured" of the problem. If you only treat the manifestations such as ulcers, blindness or blocked arteries, the patient will continue to have symptoms. To cure healthcare the patient, we must make the etiologic diagnosis and then treat it.

The Etiologic DX

I am certainly as guilty as anyone in calling healthcare a system, when it is not...systematic that is. Healthcare grew up without a plan or any unifying concepts. It was never designed. The parts of this non-system—providers, payers, patients and the government—simply had to look for themselves because there was no guidance plan of how they should behave.

Our country was founded on ideas clearly laid out in the Constitution and its Amendments. Whenever a problem arises, we can look to the governing principles to solve it. Healthcare has no such agreed-upon concepts to guide it. The fact that healthcare is a non-system pretending to be a system is why it is sick.

There are eight causes of healthcare *sickness*: eight reasons why costs keep going up; why errors keep happening; why more and more people are without insurance; why lawsuits keep multiplying; and why there are shortages of nurses and doctors.

1. Long timeline between cause and effect
2. The input *materials* are human beings.
3. Cultural confusion and ambiguity
4. Outcome measures are inappropriate.
5. Micro-economic disconnection (a new concept)
6. Mis-aligned incentives and accountability
7. Ineffectual organizational structures
8. Difficulties in managing change.

101

The Single Etiologic (Causal) DX: <u>Disconnection</u>

All eight primary diagnoses above can be summarized by one word: *disconnection.*

- Supply and demand are *disconnected* from each other and cannot balance.
- We are *disconnected* from our true purposes because three imperatives control us.
- We are *disconnected* from our most important goals because we have two masters.
- What we want is *disconnected* from what we do: incentives are disconnected from behaviors.
- We measure what we do *not* want instead of what we <u>*do*</u> want. This *disconnects* the outcomes we get from the outcomes we desire.
- Organizations *disconnect* people who <u>know how</u> from people who <u>hold power</u>.
- Feedback loops are broken–they are *disconnected.*
- The most basic of all disconnections is me from you, and you from your neighbor. We are *disconnected* from each other because we have no agreement on what we want, no consensus on principles. President Lincoln said, "A house divided against itself cannot stand." At present, healthcare is so divided – so *disconnected* – that it cannot stand.

By applying the information you acquired in the prior chapters to H.R. 3590, you can now appreciate why the Bill failed to fix or reform healthcare. It did not address the <u>disconnections</u> in healthcare.

Look carefully at the image on the front cover. I drew the tree disconnected from its roots. But healthcare is even less stable than a tree that is disconnected from its roots. *Healthcare grew up without any roots (principles) at all!*

The second part of this book will discuss what we need to do to plant healthy roots and to have a flourishing tree.

A Healthy (Healthcare) Tree

Do you get irritated when someone screams about something being wrong but then makes no suggestion of how to make it right? I do. I cannot tolerate those who tell us what is wrong with our country without showing what would be better. Part I of this book shows what is wrong with healthcare. Part II shows what we can do about it. Part I was detailed because it will provide the context and information we needed for the national dialogue suggested in the final chapter.

Healthcare is an interrelated and interdependent but dysfunctional thinking system (Chapter 4). We need to fix it but must heed the warning given by every systems thinker. If we 'fix' parts of the system separately, we will produce *fixes-that-fail-or-backfire*. H.R. 3590 was and did just that. Fixing healthcare so that it really works will require creating a totally new, uniquely American system.

Change is a often considered a dirty word. It threatens most people and because it makes them turn a deaf ear, many authors avoid the word. I cannot, not if we are going to fix healthcare. Contrast "change" with a word everyone likes: improvement. Every improvement is a change. In our own self -interest, we need to embrace change. Without change, nothing can ever be better.

Part II suggests the following. First we need to change how we think (Chapter 10). Next we need to change what we do (Chapter 11). Finally, we can change—fix—reform—cure healthcare (Chapter 12).

Reprising Jerry Maguire

In the 1996 movie *Jerry Maguire*, the lead character played by Tom Cruise, is an aggressive, unethical and unfeeling agent for high-priced professional athletes. At the beginning of the movie, Maguire has moment of self-discovery, temporarily re-defining who he is. In a night of explosive creative enthusiasm, he writes and prints 100 copies of a touchy-feely mission statement and immediately sends them off to colleagues and clients. In it, he advises more caring, more time with each client and therefore, fewer clients per agent. By the next morning, he is sorry he exposed his soft side. He lamely excuses his pamphlet apologizing with, "It was only a mission statement." He is fired the same day and that is where the film's saga begins.

> **In this chapter:**
> • Mental legacies
> • Healthcare is not…
> • Moving forward
> • Listen to the doctor

Jerry Maguire's offending pamphlet was titled "Things We Think But Do Not Say." To fix healthcare, we first need to re-think what we *know*. There is no task I can name that is harder than questioning our mental legacies yet that is exactly what we must do. If we do not think differently, we cannot act differently and then we cannot create something new and better.

Mental Legacies and *NewThink*

While some ideas and concepts from the past are still useful today, many of our mental baggage must be discarded. We tend to hold on tight to what we have and what we know. We preserve old inefficient computer systems as legacy. We treat people like machines. We look only at immediate cost. We try to control…everything. Blogger Marty Kaplan calls these out-dated, counter-productive concepts "exhausted dogmas." Exhausted dogmas should be put out to pasture. **The only legacies worth keeping are money and good will.** For the obsolete mental worse-than-useless legacies described below, a better *newthink* is suggested. (Do not confuse *newthink* with "newspeak" from George Orwell's book 1984.)

Replace the Machine Model with Systems Thinking

Nostalgia has its place...in the past. If you are looking toward the future, you have to put away the comfortable simple controllable predictable machine model.

Today we have thinking systems more than machines. They think for themselves. In thinking systems, results *emerge*. Results are not predictable: they do not "follow as the night the day."

If you stick to the machine model and the dray horse image (that needs to be whipped to move), you will never get what you want. If you can work with thinking systems and use systems thinking, then we can begin to fix healthcare, to <u>dissolve</u> (see page 114) its problems.

Problems With Perfection

Because we can produce products perfectly, we tend to believe the same about services. Intellectually, we know we are human, which means we cannot be perfect. Emotionally, we still demand perfection. Because we cannot be perfect, we do not act and become paralyzed. In the movie *Chariots of Fire*, the track runner hero justifies his perfection paralysis shouting, "I won't race if I can't win." His coach counters with, "You can't win if you don't race." When an engineer has built something that performs to specifications, but he won't release it because *I can make it better,* that is a different form of perfection paralysis. [1]

Patients expect perfect results from healthcare providers. Providers are not allowed to be human. They are blamed and shamed. [2] When they are less than perfect, we sue them for malpractice. Patients' expectation of perfection causes the practice of defensive medicine. Worse, the demand for perfection forces providers to be highly risk averse. They will follow rules and thereby protect themselves instead of using their best judgment to care for the patient.

Patients expect perfect results from healthcare providers *every time.* This presumes a guarantee than cannot be given in medicine. In the natural sciences, two plus two always equals exactly four and the speed of light is always precisely 299, 792, 458 meters per second.

In health care, ten milligrams of the same drug can have three different effects on three different people because they are different, by genetics and by how they used their bodies. Even the same person is different over time so the same dose of the same drug may affect that individual differently two years from now in contrast to today.

To expect perfect results every time is to guarantee one and only one outcome: disappointment. We need to adopt a philosophy of *perfection is the enemy of better*. Even the oft-repeated perfection is the enemy of good uses the static word "good" where we need to keep getting better and better. We always seek perfection but we know that we cannot attain it.

Control? No. Influence? Maybe.

Frederic Taylor is certainly considered one of the major forces shaping the modern industrial era. In 1911, he coined the phrase "scientific management" which was the result of time-and-motion studies. [3] Taylor sought to achieve perfect efficiency by optimizing the actions of the [human] parts of an assembly line, where the person functions as a part of a machine. There was no consideration given to the fact that the *part* was a human–with a mind of its own and free will. In a machine, a pulley is connected to a cog and their actions move a lever. The pulley doesn't get bored. The cog does not whine, "Will you stop touching me?!" The lever never comes to work drunk.

1. When you flip a light switch on the wall, an electric bulb lights up.
2. If you put your car in drive and step on the accelerator, the engine turns the axle, the axle turns the wheels and the car moves.
3. When you take a pill, you expect the pain to go away.
4. When the hospital CEO tells you to use the "Baptist Hospital System," he expects you to duplicate Baptist's success. [4]

Statements #1 and #2 are mechanical events with predictable results. You have control over the electricity or the automobile. Statements #3 and #4 relate to biologic or human systems. You do not have control. "Control" is a word left over from the machine model of the industrial age but not something you possess, even if you have authority, even if you have power. Absolute control is a mirage. Anyone who has ever raised children understands this. In today's world, you may have influence but there is no control.

The sooner we understand *Influence-yes; Control-no,* the sooner our expectations will be in sync with reality. We can then act in ways that can accomplish our goals instead of being constantly plagued with the frustration of unintended consequences.

No One Buys Goods or Services

When you buy anything, from a bowl of Cheerios to an automobile to your last will and testament, you are not purchasing goods or services. You are buying a *solution to a problem.* The cereal solves your hunger, satisfies a specific taste desire, (and Cheerios may lower your cholesterol too). The car solves your problem of getting from here to there quickly, easily and safely. With a will, you a preparing for a future problem and solving it before it happens. People do not buy products or services or even information manipulation, they buy solutions to their problems – present or future; perceived or real, makes no difference.

You buy health services for the same reason: to solve a present or future problem. Whether it is the health care you need *now* to make the pain in your belly go away, or the health insurance to get care in the *future* that won't bankrupt you, you are buying a *solution.*

The Inappropriate "Therefore"

People in healthcare believe that *we mean well–therefore we do well.* Because they do good works, the works will come out good. Unfortunately, the best intentions sometimes result in bad outcomes and the fact that providers mean well does not guarantee that we will do well.

"The road to hell is paved with good intentions." [5] Though scholars debate the identity of its original author, no one questions its accuracy. We need to discard this dangerous "therefore" entirely and ask ourselves only one question: *Can I make things better?*

People Do Not depreciate

An asset is a "useful or valuable thing, person or quality." In accounting, assets can either increase in value (appreciate) or lose value over time (depreciate). Equipment such as a medical scanner, a sewing machine or a non-vintage automobile will have less value (depreciate) over time. People are also assets but do they appreciate or depreciate?

The CEO of a highly respected New York investment house used to quip: "Our most valuable assets walk out the door every day at 5PM." Most people in management now understand that their workforce is the most important component of their company.

107

Workers add value to products and service. People (workers) innovate and improve efficiency. People are corporate as well as national assets.

Because humans learn, we increase in value over time. Because humans communicate, the learning is both shared and magnified.

People are Appreciating assets, rather than $_{de}$preciating assets.

Health Care Is Not...

There is willful ignorance as well as misconceptions and some outright fantasies about what health care be and can do. We need to clarify what health care is and what health care is not.

Health Care Is Not Health Insurance.

During the 2009 debates surrounding healthcare reform, politicians and pundits alike used the phrases health *care* and health *insurance* interchangeably as though they were synonymous. They are not. Health care is a service and health insurance is a means of paying for that service. It is important to remember that having insurance does not guarantee getting the service. What if there are no doctors or hospitals? What if the insurance payment does not cover the cost of service? What if the service doesn't exist? Furthermore, many people get health care without having health insurance.

Health Care Is Not The Practice Of Medicine

Healthcare should be a process, not a practice. Process can be defined as "a series of steps taken in order to achieve a particular end." Contrast process to the word practice: "the carrying out of a customary, habitual procedure or profession, especially that of a doctor." *Practice* focuses on what the provider does; *process* emphasizes the outcome for the customer or patient.

If healthcare were a process, it would be considered a bad one: a *malprocess*. It does deliver the outcomes we want (or at least the ones we say we want). To fix health care, we must create a functional process or system, not simply adjust practices and blame people.

Health Care Is Not A Right.

'Health-care-is-a-right' is a recent and seductive concept. Providers want to provide whatever care the patients need without reservation. The populace wants the comfort and security that puts the responsibility for their health concerns in someone else's hands. Health-is-a-right makes good fodder for sound bytes by politicians and by those appointed to positions of authority in either government or professional organizations.

Healthcare is not a right–an unencumbered privilege. All rights come automatically with responsibilities. Our Founding Fathers could not conceive things any other way.

The first ten Amendments to the Constitution–the Bill of Rights–enumerate rights that all Americans have such as: free speech (Amendment #1); keep and bear arms (#2); due process (#5); and trial by jury (#6). Each carries a responsibility. Pro-Life activists cannot prevent Pro-Choice supporters from speaking their minds. Citizens cannot use the arms they "bear" against each other. The 5th through the 9th amendments place strict responsibilities on what the Government can and cannot do. There is no such thing as a right without a responsibility.

You have the right to *hold* property but there is no right to *have* property. You have the right to *hold* your health, that is, no one has the right to make you sick. You do not the right to require someone to protect or restore your health.

Health *care* is a service provided to patients by providers. If you have a "right" to health care, you can *command* the provider to provide care. Outside the military, individuals are free to accept or reject commands and that freedom includes health care providers. To say that health care is a right would bring back slavery or at least serfdom. Health care cannot be a right.

What about the "right" to police or fire protection? Those are not rights. They are social contracts between the populace and groups of professionals. Such contracts list the responsibilities of both parties. The public must obey the legitimate orders of police or firemen and they can constrain our freedom of movement. Are there similar rules describing a patient's responsibilities in the contract with the doctor?

109

If you go hiking in the wilderness, you may became trapped or injured and need rescue. There are rangers and rescue teams contracted to do this. If, however, it is determined that you disobeyed wilderness rules and that your negligence caused the need for rescue, they still help you but you will have to pay the cost. Consider applying that principle to health care.

If you want to see what happens when there are neither social contracts nor safety nets such as MediCaid, read about health care in modern China. [6]

Health Care Is Not Passive (Or Shouldn't Be)

The doctor or nurse or healthcare system (<u>fill in your favorite villain</u>) *should keep me in good health.* Simply questioning this assertion often sets people to yelling and turns off discussion. It shouldn't. We need to discuss it.

If your health care professional, your mother, or your spiritual advisor is responsible for your health, then you are not. You are absolved of the consequences of smoking or over-eating or failing to exercise. The system including you, me, and everyone else must pay–in dollars as well as expertise and effort–for these decisions. If you are primarily responsible, then your doctor or confessor or parent is not.

Good health is not produced by the passive "delivery" of health care services. It comes from a partnership. In a recent online poll, 86% of physicians responded "No" to the question, "Is health care a right?" They know that good health can only result from an active, reciprocal relationship between doctor and patient, not the passive acceptance of "service" by client provided by a server.

Health Care Is Not Risk-Free

A core value in medicine is *primum non nocere*: first do no harm. This may have been defensible when physicians could not do much <u>good</u> but it is now actually harmful.

Defenders will say that *primum non nocere* means place the welfare of the patient first. That is not what it says or how it is used. Patients, providers, ethicists, and lawyers interpret it to mean take no risks. But patients' welfare requires risk. When the doctor advises chemotherapy for your cancer; cardiac catheterization for your coronary blockage; or just an appendectomy, she believes the risk/benefit ratio is positive and is recommending that you take that risk.

Equally important, one cannot learn without taking risks. Learning to do better for the patient requires risk to the patient during testing as well as risk to the doctor's ego and reputation by looking foolish. If "risk-free" is the prime directive, then patients will never get better from serious illness and medicine will never improve.

If you want the patient's welfare to come first, then say that. Healthcare needs a positive core value such as *primum meliorem facere* (first, help the patient get better) or *primum succurrere* (first, hasten to help), not a negative command to avoid risk.

Health Care Is Never, Ever Free

Most of us resent having to pay the doctor. At both conscious and gut levels, we believe health care should be free. Yet we also believe that things are worth what you pay for them. A Mercedes is worth more than a Kia because we are willing to pay more for the Mercedes. But if things are worth what you pay for them, what does that say about free health care?

Robert Heinlein, one of the acknowledged masters of science fiction, coined a phrase that we should all put into our everyday vocabulary. In *The Moon is a Harsh Mistress*, there is a colony of earth people on the moon analogous to Australia in the 18th century, where unwanted people were sent. In Heinlein's future, the world government shipped to the moon, first the criminals, then political activists and ultimately anyone who disagreed publicly with the status quo. [7] Out of the hodge-podge of languages in this colony of exiles, the word "*Tanstaafl*" came to be a standard greeting or ending of a conversation. It means: *There is no such thing as a free lunch.*

We have freedom in the USA. **Freedom to choose does not include freedom from the consequences of our choices.** Someone must pay for healthcare and the ultimate payer is you and me. We pay through taxes both overt and hidden. We pay for huge healthcare administrative systems–in government, private industry, insurance, and medical malpractice–that do not give us value for our dollars. We pay both personally and as a nation when there are bad medical outcomes, whether avoidable or not.

Moving Forward In Thought

Purpose and Priority

"Would you tell me, please, which way I need to walk from here?" asked
Alice.
"That depends a good deal on where you want to get to," said the Cat.
"I don't care much where-----" said Alice.
"Then it doesn't matter which way you walk," said the Cat.
[Alice in Wonderland by Lewis Carroll]

What comes first is deciding what comes first. Without a
destination, Alice will just wander and never know that she got *there*
because she never decided where *there* is.

There are many things we want from healthcare: new cures;
medical care without errors and without complications; cheap health
care; and particularly, accessible, compassionate service. Is that it? Is
that all we want? Decide! Second, what is the order of priority? We
cannot have new medical cures without risk and risk means
complications, even "errors." We have to decide which is more
important: improved care or risk-free medicine.

Try an exercise in making priorities using Russian nesting dolls
(below). Name the five dolls using healthcare priorities: Success; Safety;
Access; Personalized care; and Efficiency. Use these definitions:

- Success = best possible outcome.
- Safety = lowest risk.
- Easy access = 20-minute wait in the ER and doctor
      appointment within 48 hours.
- Personalized service = having your own preferred physician.
- Efficiency = least dollars spent and the best use of personnel
      and physical resources.

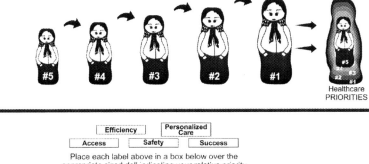

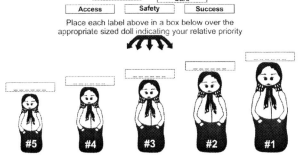

Take each preferred outcome and place it as a label on a doll. You choose which size of doll by how important that desire is to you in relation to the others: least important on the smallest doll and most desired on the biggest. This is a test with no wrong answers. There is only thing you cannot do: you cannot refuse to choose.

Not so easy, is it? Actually, it is quite difficult. You want each of these and want them equally. While you can have all five, you cannot have them in equal measure. You have to rank them in order of priority. Your choices have consequences.

If success is more important than safety, then you have to take risks to get the best possible outcome. That is not the safest course. If safety comes first, then experimental drugs and new procedures will be rejected, because they involve risk.

If efficiency is more important than personalized care, then you may accept a computer taking your history rather than a doctor. If personalized care is a higher priority, then you reject the computer history: you want and *are willing to pay for* the doctor's time.

If resource efficiency is number one, then decisions about care will be driven by cost-effectiveness analyses on populations, not individuals. Trade-offs are always necessary.

At present, there is no consensus about the priorities. Everyone wants everything equally. That is not possible. Without a consensus

113

on priorities, the system has no destination. Without a consensus, we are *Alice* wandering through Wonderland, without a destination.

Cheapest Is Not Best

While preparing a talk many years ago, I created a slide displayed to your right. My wife saw the slide and absolutely aghast, she exclaimed, "You can't show that thing! People might think you actually believe that!!"

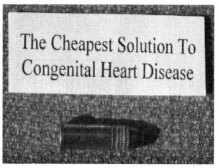

I *do* believe it. I just do not advocate it.

If short-term expenditure is your only concern, then shoot anyone with a serious condition such as heart or kidney disease. A bullet is cheaper than anything medical. Of course this is ludicrous but ask yourself: **why**? It is ludicrous because all we talk about is immediate cost while what we care about is long term health.

Most discussions about the financial problems of healthcare consider only short-term cost. In business, you do not automatically buy the cheapest materials or equipment you can find. When you think about spending money, you calculate cost and profit *in the long-term*. Will the more expensive machine last longer and be cheaper in the long run? Will the higher quality and therefore more expensive materials improve my sales and the price I can charge so that, by spending a little more now, I can make a lot more later? What effect will the quality of my goods or services have on my reputation and therefore on my ability to sell them in the future?

If a baby is born weighing less than 750 grams (1 pound 10 ounces), and dies in the delivery room, the average cost is $11, 250. If that extremely premature baby survives, the average cost for the hospitalization is $413,921. If *cheapest is best*, the deceased baby is better than the survivor. Financial calculations in healthcare do not include long-term benefit of having the live child.

What *newthink* should be use for "cost"? Change short-term line cost item analysis to <u>long-term cost/benefit</u>. An analogy with Toyota's Prius car may help our understanding.

When Toyota decided to build a fuel-efficient automobile, they started at the drawing boards. All aspects of the car's design contributed to the #1 desired outcome: fuel efficiency. It has the most aerodynamic shape possible and weighs very little. The gearing gives the most power for the least energy. The lubrication system virtually eliminates friction. Everything is *designed from the outset* to be aligned with the desired goal. The car has no contradictions or add-ons that reduce its efficiency.

Toyota did not simply insert a hybrid engine into one of their SUVs. They did not put an efficiency-robbing spoiler on the back because marketing said it might sell more cars. They started with a concept, tested to see what worked, and then built the most successful fuel-efficient car to date. The Prius is not sporty and cannot go 130 miles per hour. It will not seat six comfortably and cannot haul two tons. It does not try to be *all things to all people*.

Healthcare needs a similar approach. Healthcare needs a new system designed from scratch for a single purpose: to optimize the health and wellbeing of Americans. Period. No add-ons or qualifiers that create inefficiencies and errors. No hidden or extraneous agendas. No confusion or contradictions. THAT is not possible by modifying what we have now.

Healthcare Is Infrastructure

Infrastructure includes bridges and roads; waterways and tunnels; telephone lines, microwave towers, and satellites; and planes, trains and trucks. Infrastructure includes those elements in our country that underpin our ability to produce and to consume.

In the 18th century, our prime asset was our natural resources (and our culture). In the 19th century, it was our industrial productive capacity (and our culture). In the 20th and especially 21st centuries, it is our people and their culture. People are what underpin all our technologies and give us sustainable competitive advantage.

All successful managers know that you must take good care of your assets because they form the foundation of production and therefore of profit. To protect the productive capability of our assets, we need to pay for preventative maintenance and for repair when necessary. This is equally true whether you are talking about machines, agricultural land or people. To produce, we need functional machines, nitrogen-rich land, and healthy people. Thus, rather than simply a cost item, health care is **infrastructure support**. It is an investment in our future. [8]

Does our infrastructure make profit? Not directly. We do not want for-profit corporations in control of the bridge tollbooths. Telephone and power companies are all highly regulated. Infrastructure is not part of the market economy. It is the foundation upon the market economy makes money.

One part of healthcare, though infrastructure, makes large profits: insurance companies. They make money by withholding maintenance and repair activities that the infrastructure needs. This problem is a systemic one and can only be fixed by changing the system.

Imagine yourself as the CEO of the most successful company in the world: Corporation USA. Without a doubt, your prime asset is your people and their culture. They are your critical infrastructure. Shaky bridges, rotting foundations, and sick people are bad for business. The *healthy* child can stay in school and learn (to be productive in the future). The *healthy* 40-year old programmer or autoworker can directly and quantifiably contribute to GDP. The *still-living* elder citizen–think George Schultz and Henry Kissinger–can contribute archival memory and wisdom to our families and our nation. The dead or those in hospital beds contribute nothing.

How do you treat your prime asset, whether a natural resource, a machine or a person? You seek to maximize their function and longevity, in other words you optimize their health. For valuable machines, you would pay for both routine maintenance (preventative medicine) and repairs (sickness care) as needed. But people are more than machines: they have free will. Therefore, you would offer them positive incentives to encourage healthy behaviors.

You reward the outcomes you want from your assets: more days on the job (reduced sick days at school or at work); improved productivity (higher graduation rate; innovative computer programs; better car production); restored and sustained function after medical or surgical treatment; and longevity. *Bottom line*: as a good CEO, you would optimize and maintain your infrastructure. That means a healthy workforce. Health care becomes an investment for the future, not a line cost item.

The Four "Solves"

Russell Ackoff [9] described four ways we can handle any problem or issue. His ways are all positive. In everyday practice, people usually use negative ways to solve problems.

To absolve a problem is to grant forgiveness. The person who absolves does not change the bad outcome but forgives the person, organization or system that produced the negative impacts.

"Solve" comes from *solvere* (latin) meaning to free, release or loosen. When you solve a problem, you improve the result that would otherwise have been experienced. If your roof leaks, you can solve the problem by putting pots where the dripping occurs. That way the floor does not get wet. If a patient gets itching from a medication, you *solve* the problem by giving something that makes the itch go away.

To resolve a problem, you achieve the best possibly outcome. This is what most people seek. The leaky roof is patched so that it does not leak anymore. The doctor might switch medicines so that the new medicine does not make the patient itch.

We very rarely dissolve a problem. Dissolving a problem means that you make the problem go away, cease to exist, so that in the future, there will never be a need for absolution, solution or even resolution. You dissolve the roof leak problem by moving to a place where it does not rain. The doctor who dissolves the itchy complication cures the patient of the primary condition so that he or she does not need any medications of any kind.

Henceforth in this book, I will use the word *dissolve* to indicate an action that makes a problem or issue cease to exist. If there is no rain, then a leaky roof is functionally meaningless. If the patient needs no drugs, the fact that one medication causes itching is irrelevant.

As we should "start with our purpose in mind," what is our purpose? What we *do not* want is to absolve, resolve or even solve problems. What we *do not* want is to palliate, sedate or mesmerize. What we *do* want is to <u>dissolve</u> problems in order to <u>cure</u> healthcare.

Dissolving problems means making them go away so that they can never come back. You can *solve* hypertension by giving drugs to lower the blood pressure. You *dissolve* hypertension by eliminating the cause, such as removing an obstruction that causes the blood pressure to rise.

To dissolve problems, we need to discard linear thinking and use systems thinking.

117

Authority Commensurate With Responsibility

Too many cooks spoil the broth. Aphorisms get to be folklore because they have a kernel of truth. In healthcare, we have too many cooks without knowing who is in charge of vegetables and who cooks the meat. The result is an unpalatable meal or in medicine, bad outcomes.

Heart surgery

A surgeon was operating on a teenage girl to repair her defective heart valve. After repairing the valve, he came off bypass (meaning he allowed the heart to take up function) and evaluated the valve. As it still leaked a great deal, he decided to insert an artificial valve. When he asked for a specific sized valve, he was told that the hospital had none that size. As they were used so infrequently, that size was not stocked. After calling around, a proper valve was found in another local hospital, a technician taxied over, picked up the valve and returned to the operating institution. The valve was inserted without incident. Almost two hours of extra, unnecessary time was spent on the heart lung machine.

Heart catheterization

At the exact same time as the surgery described above, a different physician was doing a heart catheterization in a child to close a blood vessel that should have closed on its own. After measuring the size of the vessel, the doctor requested a device (a special coil made of metal) of a specific size only to be told that they had none that large. The vessel could not be safely closed at that time and the procedure was terminated. The child required a second, additional procedure.

Who is in charge of inventory and what are their priorities? Managers in technical areas are typically tasked with inventory control. While they may ask physicians for advice, they are also under orders to minimize "unnecessary" inventory.

Most times the physician does not know in advance the exact size, shape or type of valve, wire, catheter, coil, etc. that is needed in specific patient until she or he. In the vignettes above, the physician would be held legally and morally responsible for the excess time on the "pump" or the second procedure. The *responsible* physician did not have *authority* over the elements that caused the overly long pump run or the second catheterization. **To have good outcomes, you must make authority fit responsibility.**

Demand Evidence And Feedback

One of the primary reasons why things never get better is the lack of evidence and the absence of feedback. Logic alone is insufficient. It is critical to require evidence and then embed effective feedback in any decisions made, particularly by people with power over the public.

The Baldrige Award, possibly the best-known quality initiative, has been touted as an *answer* to healthcare woes. The Baldrige approach – summarized in four steps below – is effectively a demand for evidence and feedback. [10]

1. Describe exactly what you want to accomplish.
2. Indicate exactly how you will measure your results.
3. Detail the process that achieves those outcomes.
4. Confirm that what you did resulted in what you said it would.

If this approach were used in healthcare–it is not–many of the current problems would simply melt away. We would *per force* be activating an evidence-and-feedback system.

Attitude is Another Key

Recall the phrase self-fulfilling prophecy. Athletes use it to achieve the outcome they want by visualizing moves or actions in advance. If we are "hypnotized by complexity" or if we join the "consensus of futility," the result is certain: healthcare will remain just the way it is.

Let me counter the pessimists and cynics first with Clare Booth Luce–the remarkable writer, publisher and Ambassador–who wrote, "There are no hopeless situations. There are only people who have grown hopeless about them." Eleanor Roosevelt in her tireless fight for the Universal Declaration of Human Rights said, "You must do the thing you think you cannot." The attitude we should learn from these two great American women: **We can and we will because we must.**

Dee Hock developed a process where hundreds of competing banks agreed to work together. It certainly seemed impossible before he created VISA. Two quotations his book *Birth of the Chaordic Age* are particularly important when we think about fixing healthcare: "Impossibility can only be defined by the attempt" and "The sheep's first principle…Given the right circumstances, from no more than dreams, determination, and the liberty to try, **quite ordinary people consistently do extraordinary things.**" [11]

What if the Wright brothers had believed what everyone told them? What if John F. Kennedy had listened to the experts about landing on the moon? If you accept

> Optimism might be inappropriate. It certainly may not be realistic, but,
> Optimism is *absolutely necessary*.

that better and cheaper are mutually exclusive, then they are. If you grant immortality to government regulations, then we are stuck with them forever. Our expectations should be what we *want*, not what the self-styled *realists* say is possible. Some find a mantra helpful for focus and recall. If you want one, try **Stop3–Start3** in chapter note #12.

Listen to the doctor.

In *Change Your Thoughts–Change Your Life* Dr. Wayne Dyer wrote: "If you change how you think, you will change how things turn out in your life." If people change how they think, they will change their behavior. Behaviors determine outcomes. For healthcare, if both those within the industry and the general Public change how they think, we will all experience better outcomes from our healthcare system.

Uproot!

We have made the difficult internal changes including discarding outdated ideas. We have adjusted our mental models and substituted *newthink* where appropriate. Now we need to make changes beyond ourselves. We need to act.

In this chapter:
- Why change?
- Change to what?
- Information technology
- How to change?
- Healthcare on 1 page

Almost 500 years ago, Niccolò Machiavelli gave fair warning about the dangers of change. "There is nothing more difficult to take in hand, more perilous to conduct, or more uncertain in its success, than to take the lead in the introduction of a new order of things, because the innovator has for enemies all those who have done well under the old conditions and the lukewarm defender in those who might do well under the new." [1] The great novelist Dostoyevsky wrote, "Taking a new step; uttering a new word is what people fear most." Here are some of the excuses that you are likely to hear from those who wish to avoid change:

- We have been doing it this way for a hundred years. It has worked just fine and we are going to keep on doing it this way for a hundred more.
- My customers (or patients) won't know what to expect and neither will I.
- *Different Is Bad Even When It's Good.* [Commonly thought but never said out loud.]
- Better the devil we know than the one we don't.
- Every time someone makes a change, things get worse.
- We cannot afford to throw away all the investments we have already made.
- If things change, will my salary go down or my job go away?

Most of us are addicted to easy answers. We even expect them. It took 150 years to get medicine into the sorry state it is in now. [2] Is it reasonable to think anyone can fix it in one year? We must break our addition to the quick fix. There is no cure in the ten-second sound byte or a cutesy, alliterative phrase. Anyone who offers you one is selling snake oil or seeking re-election.

121

Why change healthcare?

We change because we do not like what we have or where we are. We change only when we think the change will make things better. We should not change simply for the sake of change. If you change what you are wearing, it might be an improvement: you might look or feel better, or it could make you unattractive. Change *per se* is neither good nor bad. Change is judged by its effect. Change that produces improved outcomes is good.

Healthcare has achieved a truly unenviable consensus: everyone is unhappy. According to a CBS News poll done in early 2007 and reported in *The Week*, nine out of ten Americans say that our healthcare system needs "fundamental change." Over one third (36%) say that it needs a total overhaul.

Patients complain about lack of access, high cost, inability to determine quality, and concern about errors. Caregivers—doctors, nurses and therapists—are angry about responsibility without commensurate authority; the hassle factor and heightened stress; loss of respect; and declining income. Applications to US medical schools have decreased 21% since 1996. Experienced physicians are taking early retirement and young, newly graduated doctors are leaving medicine. Nurses, pharmacists and support staff are turning over at unprecedented rates.

The consensus of unhappiness extends well beyond the general public and health care providers. Lawyers and injured patients deride the lack of consistent quality control or accepted standards, the error rate, and the perceived *conspiracy of silence* among doctors. Hospital Boards of Directors and healthcare managers view physicians as uncooperative. They see government regulations as excessive and costs as uncontrollable. Payers–insurance companies, large employers with self-insurance, and the government–raise concerns about the out-of-control upward spiral in medical costs. Businesses complain that their "profits after taxes almost equal their healthcare expenses." This makes the U.S. less competitive in the global marketplace. [3]

The short answer to "why change?" is that healthcare is a tree that is falling down and we are under it. You might just as easily ask passengers on the Titanic, "Why abandon ship?" Either we change or we will not survive (will not have health care).

Change To What?

Here is where Part I of this book comes in. You now know the diagnosis for healthcare: our so-called *system* is not systematic. There is no system in our system. Therefore, the answer to "Change to what?" is: change the non-system into a real system, one that is systematic.

The greater the change, the more threatening and the more people will resist. Healthcare is the tree we know. But we also now know that the tree has rotten roots. We need to uproot it and replace it with a healthy one, a tree with good roots. We need a totally new healthcare system.

We the People will never accept a system imposed on us, whether it is homegrown like *ClintonCare* (proposed by Hillary Clinton in 1993) or Tom Daschle's Federal Health Board [4], H.R. 3590, or imported from another country. Many have advocated adopting the systems in Canada, Japan, Germany and France. While there is much we can learn, all other systems have aspects that are unacceptable to us. [5]

We need to create our own, uniquely American system. For something as sensitive and contentious as healthcare, we will only accept something that is homegrown. The last chapter describes how that can be done.

Systems That Work Do Not Have Silos

A well-constructed system has connections between all parts. There are no silos, no isolated elements. Without connections, each part might work well separately) but the system or process will achieve nothing.

Consider a car. The engine might run smoothly with the pistons moving up and down easily but if the piston rods are not connected to the drive shaft, the car does not move. Not only do we need connections, they must be in alignment.

The piston rods might be connected to the car's driveshaft but at angles that fight against each other. This would bend the driveshaft and destroy the engine. In systems that work well the connections are aligned so that the parts work with each other and the system achieves its intended outcomes.

In healthcare, the 'parts' are disconnected. The consumer or patient does not pay (at least directly) and the payer does not consume. In economic terms, supply and demand are disconnected. In healthcare, there is actually a third party disconnected from both consumer and payer: the cost-driver, who is the doctor.

In healthcare, the system *parts* are not just mis-aligned, they actively compete with each other! Imagine one piston rod trying to take power away from another. In our current healthcare system, when the patient is sick, the doctor does well financially. When the patient needs care, payers deny care because that is how they make profit (insurance companies) or save money (government). It is hard to imagine a culture more disconnected and mis-aligned than healthcare.

If behaviors determine outcomes (they do), and the present outcomes in health care are not what we want (they are not), then we must change behaviors. That requires aligning the culture with the desired outcomes.

A highly risk-averse culture is anti-learning. The culture of management conflicts with the culture of medicine. There is mis-alignment between what is rewarded and the results we want: quoting Stephen Kerr, we want "A" but we reward "B." Healthcare culture is very rigid and therefore resistant to change, which means resistant to improvement.

We need to encourage healthcare to connect and align its culture to produce the outcomes we want. Our medical malpractice system is an excellent example of how a disconnected and mis-aligned system fails to achieve the outcomes we want

In the US *criminal* legal system, a person is presumed innocent until proven guilty. In the US *medical malpractice* system, the provider is guilty until proven innocent (if that is even possible). The entire system is based on tort law and makes adversaries out of the people who should be allies. It disconnects doctor and patient. Patients want the med-mal system to protect them and to compensate them when injured. It does neither because the system is mis-aligned. The proper *fix* is to align it. The new system should not have silos called Plaintiff and Defendant and should not consider risk a dirty word. The new system should:

- Protect patients from bad outcomes, whether due to a mistake or not.
- Help patients when adverse outcomes occur without assigning blame.
- Encourage learning (risk-taking) because that produces better outcomes.

Simplify!

Whether you look at the success of Toyota Production Systems [6] or just talk to managers in any successful business, one message is clear. Complexity costs money and increases errors. A system that works well is simple, easily understood and has free information exchange. Effective designers and managers reduce complexity to a minimum.

Complexity is most commonly seen as the number of steps or links in a process. The more steps there are, the greater chance for error, for cost and waste, and the greater the need for reconciliation. Effective approaches to error-reduction start with reducing complexity. A process that requires five people to get a drug to a patient introduces five different opportunities to go wrong. If the same person orders, gets and administers the drug, there is no possibility of miscommunication.

Complexity can "kill" patients by delaying appropriate care; by providing the wrong care; by introducing errors; and by costing so much that it starves the useful parts of the care system. Every estimate suggests that 30-40% of the healthcare dollar goes to the bureaucracy. Complexity and bureaucracy function like a positive feedback loop. As one grows so does the other, each expanding the other.

An ancient Chinese torture method was called the Death of a Thousand Cuts. Each cut was short and superficial but the sum of all the incisions was exquisitely painful and caused the victim to bleed to death. Many nurses and doctors feel that they are enduring a bureaucratic Death by a Thousand Cuts every day at work. As the bureaucracy expands, providers' ability (and willingness) to do what is right for the patient *regardless of rules and regs* gets inundated and lost.

The old saw about a camel being a horse designed by a committee is true of almost everything in healthcare. Most mandates are designed by congressional committees whose members have no understanding of what their mandates do in the real world. Mandates are passed with neither preliminary testing nor consideration of how the mandate affects other parts of the process. There is no automatic feedback and no long-term cost/benefit analysis. To be blunt, no one thinks in terms of a process, just their own little silo, and no one thinks about the cumulative effect on healthcare of all the silos. Look at the doctor and his backpack.

The Doctor and his Backpack

With his permission, I will share work done by a colleague along with his illustration (Chapter note #8). David Dilts is an engineering expert at the Owen Graduate School of Management at Vanderbilt University. He applied his operations expertise to study how biomedical research is done at his Center. David did not investigate the quality or quantity of the research, just the process by which it is done at Vanderbilt and presumably at most academic medical centers.

It came as a shock that the process of investigator-initiated biomedical research required 87 separate steps and committee approvals! By training, Dr. Dilts is an engineer. This process offended his engineer's commitment to simplicity, efficiency and elegance. In this "system," there were nine stopping points, each of which made the investigator start all over again. There were 15(!) additional steps are required <u>after</u> the project is approved. While any one step or committee might be justifiable, the process as a whole is redundant and inefficient, with a strongly negative cost/benefit ratio. It cries out for radical change.

Undoubtedly, one of the hardest areas to simplify will be the legal and regulatory. Probably the most effective way to handle this issue is a new law that simply says healthcare regulations, laws and mandates will automatically sunset (be canceled) within five years unless they can demonstrate a long-term positive cost benefit analysis.

Reconciliation Is the Devil

We constantly hear that the House and Senate versions of some legislation must go to committee for *reconciliation*–to make them compatible. In business, reconciliation is routinely used to correct inconsistencies and mistakes. When production makes 100 blue cars, but Sales wanted 80 blue and 20 red, someone must reconcile the difference.

If the House and Senate worked together in the first place to draft the Bill, reconciliation would be unnecessary. If the sales people controlled the colors of automobiles during production, no one would have to find 20 more red cars and unload 20 unwanted blue ones. Even better, to avoid unnecessary checks, to reduce redundant controls and to eliminate the need for reconciliation, put controls where they really should be. For car color, have the *customer* control the color during production.

In their seminal book *Reengineering the Corporation,* Hammer and Champy argue against checks, controls and reconciliation. In their condemnations, they spared healthcare probably to be kind. You and I cannot afford to be kind. Healthcare is replete with reconciliation steps that are required by an overly complex and excessively regulated system…and we must pay for them.

Reconciliation is the *devil.* It is an admission of a bad process. If we do it right the first time and every time, there is no need for reconciliation. If the system were designed to make things compatible and right *during* the planning process, there would be no need for reconciliation. Rather than adding value, reconciliation adds cost, time and a new source for errors. Reconciliation is deadweight, a sign of a poorly constructed process.

The <u>System</u> Protects The Patient

The doors of our police cars read: "To serve and protect." Our healthcare system could learn from the police.

Providers are human and therefore imperfect. They make mistakes and some of these mistakes hurt patients. The system should protect us rather than depending on and expecting what does not exist: perfect providers.

Rather than being encouraging systematic protections, providers, the bureaucracy, even the patients resist the application of error-proofing, FMEA, and standardization to name but a few proven techniques. Some of the reasons for resistance to standardization are suggested in chapter note 9.

There is a great potential for improvement using system-wide protection. That potential includes both better, safer medical outcomes and huge cost reduction. One specialty in medicine–Anesthesiology–implemented error-reducing techniques from industry and dropped their complication rate by over 90%.

The Public needs to demand that **the system** protect them both from the reality that providers are human and from the fact that medicine does not have all the answers. The Public also needs to empower the healthcare system, not the regulatory bureaucracy, to create, test and implement those protections. Compliance with regulations from Washington does not necessarily translate into a safe hospital stay.

Healthcare must learn what protects us and what does not. That knowledge must be shared across State lines. To have a healthcare culture that learns requires radical reform of the medical malpractice system (see Appendix I) and a national medical information system.

Information Technology: Blessing & Curse

Much has been written recently about how information technology (I.T.) can rescue healthcare, reduce inefficiency as well as errors, and save literally billions of dollars.

I.T. is both a blessing and a curse. Is a computer the *answer* to anything? No, a computer is an enabler, something that can help us do more, better, faster and offers new options, like video conferencing. Computers enable both good things as well as bad: sharing digital x-rays pictures but also facilitating pornography and terrorism.

The Blessing First

When implemented properly, I.T. can improve health care, reduce errors, facilitate communication, reduce hassle, and save money. Better and cheaper are *not* mutually exclusive. I.T. can reduce worker frustration. In turn, this would lead to higher retention and ultimately better outcomes: higher quality, less cost, and fewer adverse impacts.

The epidemiologic advantages could be profound. A fully interoperable national healthcare I.T. system would allow bio-surveillance against both terrorist biologic attacks and natural epidemics such as bird or swine flu. With such a system, responses could be more rapid and effective in the event of any disaster. If a radiation leak occurred, a national I.T. system could identify all facilities capable of treating such victims and the means to transport them.

Walker studied the financial implications of a national healthcare I.T. system. [10] Over ten years' implementation, it would *cost* >$270 billion dollars and would *save* >$600 billion! When fully operational, the estimated net savings would be $77.8 billion per year. This represents 5% of projected total annual U.S. spending on healthcare.

Walker also showed that *partial* implementation of an I.T. system would actually lose $34 billion during the implementation. This provides another example of the all-or-nothing principle: incremental moves, baby steps, *working into it slowly* will not work in a system so completely interdependent as healthcare.

Now The Curse

Information technology can also be a curse, particularly if it fails to deliver as needed. There are four reasons why I.T. can be a curse:

1) *We can therefore we do;*
2) Change slowly, by increments;
3) Programmers; and
4) Lack of user input.

The very great capability of computers and information technologies tempts us to acquire more and more data, because we can analyze it and store it easily. As a result, we analyze too much. We spend million of hours generating reports, many not worth the time – time that could be better spent with the patients for doctors and nurses, or with the doctors and nurses for managers. *We can* [track and calculate] *therefore we do* is one of the many seductive siren calls that we must resist if I.T. is to fulfill its promise.

Legacy systems are a big part of the I.T. curse. For instance, suppose you already had programs in place for Radiology, Cardiology, and Laboratories, and you wanted to implement a patient-scheduling program. Keeping the old, separate systems and adding another, simply compounds the complexity; demands additional translation programs; or worse, requires people who must reconcile the communication glitches. Without a fully integrated system, scheduling could set up an appointment for a heart patient when there is no doctor available, when the echo lab is booked, or when Radiology is down for routine maintenance.

At every hospital I have ever visited, the power of legacy prevails. Management looks at the millions already spent and refuses to throw away their *investment.* The excuse is always *too big and too expensive.* Legacy I.T. systems actually make health care more costly and more dangerous.

The computer programmer of today is like the engineer in the 1950's: mesmerized by possibilities. Because he can make it a little better, do a little more, and add even more buttons, he does. After all, he thinks: *who doesn't want to have more choices?*

I bet you are just like me. At our home, we have four separate handheld controllers for the TV, DVD, amplifier, and cable box. They have, respectively, 42, 44, 45 and 61 buttons. Do I really need 192 buttons to watch a movie on TV? A properly implemented I.T.

system does *not* mean more programs with greater capability, more options, and a multitude of buttons, icons and decisions. It means **serving the needs of the end-user.**

HOW To Change (Implementation)

The **extent** of change depends on a) what result you want, and b) the extent to which the present system fails to achieve those results. While the USA has some of the finest providers in the world and certainly is the most medically innovative country, [11] *as a system*, U.S. healthcare is a failure. Thus the necessary extent of change is replacement–uproot the dying tree and plant good roots for a new healthy one.

The optimal **speed** of change is counter-intuitive and contrary to what most textbooks advise. Organizational theorists intone that systems do not like change and need time to adapt. The first part is true and the last is…disingenuous. Systems are like our bodies: they want to survive *exactly as they are*: <u>unchanged</u>. Systems "adapt" to change by watering it down, delaying and preventing change, all to protect the status quo.

The greater the extent of change necessary, the FASTER you need to move forward. If you make change incrementally, the system has time to organize its resistance and counter each little baby step so that the big change never happens.

The **people involved** in change can be divided into three groups: drivers, resistors, and those affected. The drivers or agents of change are never popular no matter how necessary the change. By recommending change, people assume the change advocate is saying those who came before did things wrong. Change agents are considered not only threatening but disloyal.

The agents must recognize that their role will be unpopular. Even as they work to improve things for all, they must accept that when the change process is firmly in place, they need to leave.

Organizational research [12] has taught us that you facilitate change more by reducing the resistance than by increasing the force behind the driver. Put differently, effective drivers of change spend most of their time dealing with, attenuating, countering, and preferably enlisting those who resist the change. You catch more fly with honey than vinegar (assuming you *want* to catch flies!)

Change Requires Balancing Drivers and Resisters

Dr. W. Edwards Deming, a pioneer in the improvement movement, had two basic rules of life: 1) Change is inevitable; and 2) Everyone resists change. Even when resisters know they must adapt or die, they still cling to the status quo and work against change.

There is no single answer or *one way* to deal with resistance except to avoid making it personal (even when resistors do). If the change agent lets it become you-versus-me, then the personal conflict takes over, drowning out how change can make things better. You see this every day when people "discuss" healthcare. Both sides of an issue, say Healthcare Reform in 2009, make personal attacks on individuals and parties instead of sticking to the issue: how to fix a sick healthcare system.

Usually, **the affected** are those who play no role in the change but are "affected" by it. In the case of reforming healthcare, the affected– that is you, me and everyone else: the Public–need to take on a different role. We must participate in the change process. Indeed, we-the-affected need to become the initiators of change.

Planning change always starts, as Stephen Covey wrote, "with the end in mind." [13] We should start with what we want as an outcome, NOT what is considered possible, NOT what the budget will allow, and NOT bound by our legacies. We know that results will *emerge* rather than be completely predictable, but that is the nature of thinking systems.

A long timeline and the lack of absolute predictability should not be used as excuses to avoid change. To achieve improvement, we must resist perfection paralysis and accept that we can influence the future positively but we cannot control it.

People sometimes confuse the finished tool with the final outcome. The completed Venn diagram, operational flow chart, or trend analysis is not what we want. Total Quality Management, Toyota Production Systems, Internal Customer Concept, and systems thinking are management philosophies. We want results, not tools or philosophies. Avoid confusion about desired outcomes. We want to be healthy and care little about the tools providers use to make us so.

Healthcare On One Page

The first ten Amendments to the US Constitution–the Bill of Rights–are the fundamental founding principles of our country. They take up less than one page. Over the years, Congress tried to be more specific and exert more control. For healthcare, this produced confusion, unnecessary complexity, contradictions, and costs. AND, we failed to realize the outcomes intended by the legislation. Read about UMRA and HIPAA.

Look up *ClintonCare* (1993) or H.R. 3590: the first is over 1000 pages long and the second is well over 2300! When Congress micromanages anything, some results are absolutely guaranteed: more complexity, increased bureaucracy, inefficiency, and cost.

Lawmakers are not the right people to design a workable healthcare system. Neither is the public. The way to deal with our failing system is for the Public to enunciate basic principles. Congress should then empower groups of experts to design a system based on those principles. These groups would include providers, public advocates, management experts including systems thinkers, financiers, and as few lawyers as possible. Exclude anyone who needs to get re-elected.

The principles should be simple and straightforward, requiring no more than one page. Take a minute and write down *your* thoughts for the guiding principles you want for healthcare. Avoid qualifiers, just like the Bill of Rights. Try it on the next page.

<u>*My*</u> **Personal Healthcare Principles**

1.

2.

3.

4.

5.

6.

Plant Good Roots

Up to this point, everything has been background, important theory, and laying the foundation. Now it is time for action: here is what we must do to get what we need.

In this chapter:
• Demand Value
• Fixing healthcare
• The "Cure"

Demand Value For Your Healthcare Dollar

Things always seem to start with money even though money is not the *bottom line* for healthcare. The real bottom line is our health (and healthy people generate money). As we now know, we need to talk about getting **value**–positive cost/benefit–for the money we spend on healthcare. How do we do this?

Start with the denominator: benefits. We must demand that healthcare measure and track the positive outcomes we want, rather than the negative ones they currently follow, which are the outcomes we do not want. For the numerator – costs – we must distinguish costs we want to pay for, such as those that produce better health and living longer, from those that are not worth the expense or are just plain waste.

Costs We Want To Pay	Costs We Want To Eliminate
1. New treatment options (New Value)	3. Action without evidence
2. More people living longer	4. Bureaucracy, Inefficiency, Reconciliation, and Regulatory burden
	5. Micro-economic disconnection
	6. Perverse incentives
	7. Defensive medicine
	8. Adverse outcomes and errors
	9. Money taken out of healthcare
	10. Fraud and embezzlement

135

The old system of healthcare financing was fee-for-service for doctors and cost-plus for hospitals. It was rejected because it encouraged *unnecessary* medical care. It was replaced by fixed payments and managed care, or as Klienke calls it "managed cost." [1] Managed care discourages *needed* medical care and again fails to get us what we want. Therefore:

- We should not return to the old way of financing healthcare.
- We should not try to adjust the current system.
- We should create a new healthcare financing system that offers incentives to produce the outcomes we want.

Is this hard? Yes, certainly. Is it what we must do? Yes, if we want a system that *works for us*. If we simply tinker with the current system, we will still be here in twenty years with the same complaint: our healthcare system does not work.

A glance at "Costs We Want To Eliminate" on the right side of the previous Table shows we can save hundreds of billions of dollars without losing value. **To get value for our healthcare dollar, we need to change processes, systems and culture, rather than blame people, parts and custom.**

We could start by demanding that all laws, mandates and regulations have The same three features that are required when practicing good medicine: 1) proof-of-effect; 2) cost/benefit analysis; and 3) real feedback to the legislators who pass them. That alone would save hundreds of billions in #3, 4, 5, 6 and 8 in the above table. An inter-operable health information system that includes error-prevention and simplified billing will reduce wasteful costs in #5, 7, 8, and 10. The question of profits taken out of healthcare (#9) is left open, subject to national discussion and decision.

Seven Steps To Fix Healthcare

We all tend to judge the message by the messenger. If someone we really detest says the sky is blue, we think green or more likely do not hear the person at all. The author—me—is a physician. You may tend to believe that what I write is because of who I am. If I defend doctors or nurses, you think, *that is just one of them protecting their own.*

I plead with you to consider the message and not the messenger. It is the substance of my words I ask you to judge, not where I grew up or what I do for a living. Imagine that the author is Dana Smith, about whom you know absolutely nothing, not even gender.

1. Accept the job and our role

We must accept the fact that our *broken* healthcare system cannot be fixed. We need a new one – a homegrown, Built-in-USA system, not an import imposed on us. Whether it is a broken axle on your car or a heart that is irreparably damaged, you do not use a welder or continue pain-killers, you replace what cannot be fixed. Healthcare cannot be fixed. The problem is the system: there is no "system." It has no founding principles.

Our role is healer. For healthcare, that means uprooting the dying tree and planting one with good roots. No one else can do it. Only the Public can do what is necessary.

2. Demand a dialogue

The healing process starts with an extended, organized dialogue: us listening to the experts discuss and debate. Then we need to talk amongst ourselves. This must be a nation-wide activity involving every level of our society. (I hope to publish this book in languages other than English to ensure that Spanish so that the large segments of our population will not be disenfranchised.) Such a dialogue requires leadership by and organization from Washington. Anything less will fail to produce what we need: a consensus on principles for the new system (see #4 below).

The national dialogue will use every possible mode of communication: the internet from blogs on Huffington Post to Twitter; town hall meetings–thousands of them; print media such as newspapers and magazines; and certainly radio as well as TV.

In the 1970s, Fred Friendly [2] ran a series of public TV broadcasts called *Ethics in America*. He would gather a large and highly diverse group of people to discuss topics of interest and controversy, from abortion to eminent domain to asking if war can ever be ethical? The purpose was not to push any single view but to explore diverse opinions for the audience's consideration.

I hope to see hundreds of televised debates on topics such as:
- "Should there be a safety net and if so, how big a net?"
- "If everyone is able to get insurance, should the ER refuse care to a person who chooses not to have insurance?"
- "How can we reconnect us with our own dollars?"
- "Who makes the ultimate decisions about my care?"
- "What do we want medical malpractice to DO?"
- "Does competition in health care services benefit the patients?"
- "What should be the status of residents-not-here-legally in our healthcare system?"
- "Should there be profit in health care and if so, where?"

I would expect that each such debate to be subsequently published and form the basis of town hall meetings around the country. As the President of the National Coalition on Health Care recently said, "We need a big debate on how to get a grip on [and what to do with] this system!" [3]

That there will be much anger and venting is certain. Change is frightening. We need to look at this phase of the healing process as grieving. Not only is the old system is dying to make way for the new, better one, [4] but we are helping it along–we are *uprooting* the dead tree.

The great Dr. Elisabeth Kübler-Ross described five phases of grieving in preparation for death. [5] She emphasized that people need to go through the first four in order to get to peace. The following applies her five stages to the healing of healthcare.

Stage 1: Denial (*Healthcare can't be that bad.*)

Stage 2: Anger (*I'm furious with the doctors or insurance companies or the government or….*)

Stage 3: Bargaining (*If I don't complain too much, maybe I can get care.*)

Stage 4: Depression (*Why bother? I'm going to die whatever I do.*) Both the organizers of and the participants in our national dialogue must recognize that the public needs to go through all four stages before getting to Stage 5.

Stage 5: Acceptance (*I guess we can get together and make it work.*)

3. Communicate and learn

We need to learn from the experts and even more from each other. We must communicate with each other, often and over a long period of time. We will have to go through Dr. Kubler-Ross' stages above. Eventually we will form a consensus on what we want our new healthcare system to do.

It is during this national conversation that the first half of this book will be particularly useful, helping us communicate effectively with each other. We will have a common language. We understand that we need to re-connect–payer with consumer and incentives with outcomes–and after Part I, we understand why. We now know the right questions that WE need to answer in discussion with our selves.

We the Public will not accept anything imposed on us by Washington, including some other country's healthcare system. Our Government needs to accept the following management wisdom: *If we don't own it, we won't buy it.*

The national dialogue process must be organized and facilitated by Washington. The outcome will not be in its control, or the AMA's, or the control of any special interest. The ultimate result–the consensus–will be evident through step #5 below.

4. Create a consensus

We need to discuss all those *politically incorrect* questions that those in Washington wants to avoid. Anyone who raises such questions will alienate some part of the voting public and that is why you hear nothing from the politicians about health care for illegal residents, personal responsibility, or paying the doctor directly. Nonetheless, we cannot have a healthcare system without answers to the sticky, polarizing questions.

After talking and more talking, yelling and debating, arguing and cajoling, specific views, solutions, and answers will become dominant. Certainly each of us will hear all sides of issues and develop our own opinions based on the evidence. We will create a consensus that needs to be heard.

5. Speak with one voice

The consensus about what healthcare should do must be clearly communicated to the Federal government. That consensus will form the guiding principles for our new system, a system built on what the majority decides.

As part of the "demand" we made back in step #1, we had to require an end-point for our dialogue punctuated by a plebiscite, from Latin: *plebes* or common people + *scitum* meaning decree of. It literally means we have a national vote, like an election but we vote on an issue not on individuals.

The national vote or plebiscite should consist of no more than 10 questions constructed so that our answers form the basic principles, the guiding ideas, for a new healthcare system.

6. Demand a "Death Panel"

Not for people of course, but for rules and regulations. We all do cost-benefit analysis before we make a decision. We expect our doctor to have evidence and show it to us before operating. Why shouldn't government have the same obligation?

This is simple. I cannot imagine anyone disagreeing (except people in Washington). Create a Commission that acts similarly to the base-closing hearings for the military. I over-dramatized by calling it a "Death Panel," so let's call it the Sunset Commission.

The Sunset Commission should have the power to require all Federal agencies that regulate healthcare to submit a cost/benefit analysis every three years. If the Sunset Commission finds that the proven benefit to the public is not worth the cost to the public, than it should cut off funding.

7. Accept or Reject

Following the plebiscite, the Federal government will be tasked with creating a new healthcare system based on the principles we agreed to in the plebiscite. During this time, the current system will remain in effect. The new system will be accepted or rejected in a second national vote two years after the plebiscite.

8. A process with partners

The Public understands that whatever the specifics are of the new healthcare system, it will not work unless there is a *process with partners*, in essence multiple partnerships of person with: doctor, organization and especially country.

We need to discard the old idea of the doctor healing the patient. Preserving–and when sick restoring–our health is a lifelong process of patients in partnership with processes. Of course the cultural healing elements must be preserved: fiduciary relationship, trust in the doctor-leader (of the team), and reaffirmation of healthcare's prime directive: patient welfare comes above all else. However, modern health care is composed of processes, not mom-and-pop silos.

Having a health care partnership means we must give up the phrase health care *delivery*. The word "delivery" indicates that one person gives while another receives. The first person is actively *doing* while the second is passively *accepting*. Good <u>health</u> (notice I did not write health <u>care</u>) cannot be *delivered*. Patient and provider must commit to each other in order to optimize patient health.

Healthcare should also foster partnering between providers and managers, bridging the GAP. [6] Organizationally, medical schools should partner with business schools to their mutual advantages.

As a populace, we must partner with each other, understanding that healthcare is not a zero-sum game or win-lose scenario. You, our neighbors, and I can all win.

We must partner with the place where we work (and it must partner with us). People are *ap*preciating assets, both for our organizations and our nation.

We are the most important component of U.S. infrastructure. We provide competitive advantage to our nation as long as we are healthy and there are many of us. Therefore, the Government "wins" by keeping us healthy. That is the largest and most important partnership: a healthy us for a healthy U.S.

The *Cure*

On an episode on the *West Wing*, a group of doctors visiting the White House muse over the fact that with enough resources they could cure cancer. The President, played by Martin Sheen, overhears them and says: "Talk to me." The hour-long episode centers around what it would take and ultimately why political reality makes this impossible. As a nation, we must reject such so-called political reality.

Together, we can cure U.S. healthcare. This requires:

- A Public that understands <u>why</u> healthcare does not work.

- A Public that knows what it wants <u>healthcare to do</u> for them, and

- Has created a <u>consensus</u> about healthcare's guiding principles.

- A Public that will *Uproot* sickly U.S. healthcare and will

- Plant good roots–guiding <u>principles</u>–for a *uniquely American system*.

- A Public that will <u>partner</u> with the new system to achieve better *health*–not just health *care*–for all.

- We know that a healthy populace means a more <u>successful USA</u>.

- This knowledgeable Public can distinguish empty promises from <u>effective change</u> and **<u>will accept nothing less</u>**.

Chapter Notes

Chapter 1: We *Always* Learn.

1.   In the 1940s, *Life* magazine advertised the health benefits of cigarette smoking.

2.   In citation #118, Coutu reports her interview with the widely respected consultant Edgar Schein who believed that people strongly resist learning. His view is diametrically opposite of Peter Senge (cit. 434), who wrote that people love to learn.

3.   See the fascinating works by Ackoff, Beinhocker, Johnson, McDaniel and others cited as references #4, 39, 46, 235, 254, 255, 289, 326, 327, 469, 470, and 515.

4.   The hierarchy of human goals was initially explicated by Maslow (cit. 320), a fascinating person in his own right.

5.   I always thought Bruner's definition of creativity (cit. 78) was perfect: "Figuring out how to use what you already know in order to go beyond what you currently think."

6.   Everett Rogers who just recently died was a revered and much loved Professor at my own University. His book <u>Diffusion of Innovation</u> (cit. 416) is heavy reading but fascinating.

7.   In order to calculate the cost of turnover, Mobley (cit. 353) had to study the rate at which people learned until they achieved "job mastery." He did this in the Bell Telephone System of the 1970s, hence the reference to climbing up telephone poles.

8.   See citation #117 that details the application of air industry safety procedures to medicine.

9.   Our work on retention – citations 507-9, 512, and 513 – showed that net five-year retention of doctors was 45% and of nurses was 17%. From a patient's standpoint, this should be terrifying. It means that your nurse is unlikely to know all those little things about your hospital that make the difference between an easy, successful admission, and errors or inefficiency leading complications and wasteful health care.

10. There is a large body of information confirming the volume-to-outcome relationship. This is also true in medicine. Some useful citations are the following: 38, 51, 52, 95, 153, 200, 240, 268, 305, 330, 391, 456, and 523. Additional references on this subject can be found in our citation 507.

11. We applied learning curve theory to healthcare in citations 506 and 514.

12. The whole subject of learning how to learn is fascinating and worth your time, whether you are parents of school age children or just someone who wants to be an involved citizen. Some of the citations you might start with are: 118, 163, 181, 376, 434, 470, 506, and 514.

Chapter 2: Broken Loops

1. Messinger et al (cit. 338) reported follow-up studies in children born to cocaine-addicted mothers.

2. George Bernard Shaw had a particular grudge against the doctors of his day and expressed it bitingly in his famous Preface to *The Doctor's Dilemma* (cit. 440). If you ever want a scathing quote to put down doctors, this is your source.

3. It is astonishing to me that the phrase "evidence-based medicine" (cit. #97) is less than fifty years old!

4. The following publications discuss the development of evidence-based decision-making in the practice of medicine: #7, 15, 16, 19, 20, 26, 38, 47, 48, 52, 92, 120, 143, 151, 153, 182, 193, 200, 221, 228, 271, 281, 284, 328, 330, 342, 355, 391, 416, 422, 452, and 526.

5. The quote comes from Axelsson (cit. #26) credited with introducing the term scientific management into healthcare.

Chapter 3: *Malprocess*, not Malpractice

1. See citation 117 for how error-reduction techniques proven in aviation can be adapted to medicine.

2. See Keeton's textbook on Torts (not the kind you eat; these eat you): citation 257.

3. Supreme Court Justice Learned Hand explicated negligence as follows. When the **cost** (in whatever terms – money, time, preparation, prior training) is less than the likelihood of something bad happening multiplied by the amount of damage that occurs.

    $$Cp < (p*L) \text{ where:}$$

    Cp = cost of prevention (\$)
    p = probability of loss or injury
    L = loss due to a negligent act (\$)

    o   Note that loss (L) is expressed strictly in monetary terms, requiring dollar valuation of a human life or of pain, emotional distress or loss of function.

    o   The first consequence of Justice Hand's definition is that, as the amount of possible damage increases, there is greater obligation to prevent. In other words, little needs to be spent to prevent a broken fingernail but much should be expended to prevent death.

    o   The reverse corollary is that there may be conditions where it does not 'pay' to prevent an injury. [Automobile makers commonly use this calculation to decide whether or not to perform a recall on a defective car component.] Learned Hand countered this *simple calculus* writing, "Courts must in the end say what is required; there are precautions so imperative that even their universal disregard will not excuse their omission." Thus, Justice Hand, for the Court, said that not everything is a simple, monetary calculation: cost of the recall versus cost of the lawsuits. For some things such as *knowing* that the gas tank in a Pinto will explode, there is no appropriate calculation. The responsible person should just do the right thing and the Court will decide guilt or innocence if a bad thing happens.

4.   If you, the reader, are related to healthcare in any way you NEED to read the Bristol Report (www.bristol-inquiry.org.uk/final_report/index.htm.) to see how highly trained, well-meaning people can do terrible things because of a system that does not work.

5.   Some writers start by wanting to prove their bias like *all lawyers are evil; doctors bury their mistakes;* or the *insurance companies are bloodsucking vampires.* From them we can learn little that is useful. However, there is much useful published data in citations: 67-71, 92, 96, 125, 126, 217, 253, 278, 286, 290, 294, 300, 337, 371, 374, 411, 429, 435, 478, 483, 484, 493, 503, and 542.

6.   Citation 427 describes a Wyoming case where insurance decisions were ruled the practice of medicine.

7.   Jerome Groupman's book titled *How Doctors Think* (cit. 192) explores the reasons for medical cognitive dissonance from the personality traits of providers to personal interactions with patients. He also suggests some proactive ways both doctors and patients can improve thinking and protect ourselves.

8.   Many see Lucian Leape's 1994 article *Error in Medicine* (cit. 290) as a great clarion call about quality problems in U.S. medicine. Then view the problem from the non-physician perspective in citation 91.

9.   Ms Claybrook's opinion piece is citation 96.

10.   Some truths appear from a literature search on frequency of claims and monetary consequences. "An award payment to a plaintiff is not a direct indicator that malpractice has occurred." (cit. 92) Forty percent of incidents reported by physicians to insurance companies are never pursued by the patient. From 1970 to 1986, the frequency of claims filed increased over 400%, mostly related to changes in the law. In 1987, the cost of our tort system for med-mal was estimated at $117 billion, which was 2.5% of U.S. GDP. This is 3-8 times the corresponding cost in Europe. "The relationship between injuries caused by negligence and medical malpractice claims can be described as both lopsided and mismatched."(cit. 478)
      In one large California study, birth injury cases were by far the most expensive claims, accounting for 78% of all indemnities paid. Only 28% of the med-mal premium dollar goes to the injured patient and the average time to closure of a case is 4-5 years (cit. 371) – an eternity for physician and patient alike.

11.   Citation #126 is another of the excellent reports coming out of Rand Corporation.

12.   In our 2003 article on med-mal (cit. 503), we showed that children are treated different in med-mal. Providers are presumed guilty rather than innocent. After all, *children should never die so someone must be to blame.*

13.   Tim Garson (cit. #169) wrote, "We must define quality and measure it."

14. In their best-selling book *Freakonomics*, Levitt and Dubner (cit. 295) gleefully describe many perverse outcomes, where you would logically expect one result and the opposite occurs. Prices rose after deregulation of the energy industry. In systems thinking, such results are called "policy resistance." Whatever label you prefer – *Freakonomics*, policy resistance, counter-intuitive results, or Murphy's Law – the concept is very important. What happens is often the opposite of what was expected.

15. For those interested in exploring how healthcare handles medical errors, the following is provided.

Error	Information	Citation #
Classifications	• Over-use, under-use, mis-use. • Fail to order, monitor, or do; delay; improper work-up • Systemic versus Individual: skill-based, rule-based, or knowledge-based	290 278 328
Are identified if:	Visible impact *and* Willingness to report	151
	The person who reports the error feels responsibility either to the patient or to fulfilling the reporter's duty.	542
Defensive strategies	(1) Shoot the messenger. (2) Distort or suppress the data. (3) Blame someone else (anyone but me!)	47
Ways to handle errors	Complete honesty in communication	542 & 277
	Convert to a *benign* failure	193
	• **P** artnership of all stakeholders • **R** eporting errors without blame • **O** pen-ended focus groups • **C** ultural shift • **E** ducation and training programs • **S** tatistical analysis of error data • **S** ystem redesign.	328

16. Following is a detailed explanation of money flow into and out of the med-mal system

Dollars *going into* the med-mal system can be broken into the following.

  • Liability insurance premiums paid by doctors and hospitals, estimated at $10-15 billion per year;

  • Self-insurance paid by hospitals, probably $2-5 billion;

  • Payments for covering uninsured malpractice losses, estimated at over $4 billion;

- Court costs, for which there is no good estimate;
- Money spent on defensive medicine: any estimate would be a WAG ("wild-assed guess").

How do insurance companies determine the amounts they charge for med-mal premiums? These amounts have absolutely no relationship to what the injured patient needs (disconnection again). They have no relation to the quality of medicine practiced. Thus med-mal fails at its two stated purposes.
Med-mal insurance premiums are based what a company estimates it will pay out considering the following factors. Note that the injured patient's needs have no bearing on the calculation.

- Location of event: Higher payments must be made in certain areas compared to others. A Government Accounting Office study showed that physicians paid $4, 359 per year for malpractice premiums in Nebraska, $21, 764 in rural Illinois and in Chicago, the price was $48,718 each year. One would assume that the best doctors are in Nebraska and one should avoid getting sick in Chicago.
- Specialty practiced: Obstetricians get sued more often and are liable for longer periods of time (age of maturity of their patients, i.e., 21 years!) than internists. Is it any wonder that fewer and fewer graduating medical students are choosing Obstetrics and that it is harder every day for a pregnant women to find a physician to deliver her baby?
- Demographics of the physician: women get sued less frequently than men; Neurosurgeons more than Emergency Medicine doctors.
- Prior history in that jurisdiction: Lawyers for both Plaintiff and Defendant study the history of prior tort cases in the jurisdiction where the trial will be held. This is an important datum when planning their strategy. Some Courts are known to favor doctors and others have given huge awards to plaintiffs. For example, there was the infamous multi-million dollar award given to the woman burned by very hot coffee after she placed the open cup between her legs in a moving car. Such a venue would be favored by plaintiffs' attorneys.

After the initial phases of the lawsuit, the defendant insurance company makes a calculation: (A) Cost of defending the case versus (B) Cost and likelihood of a judgment against them compared to (C) What they can settle for. The insurance company then makes a decision. Right and wrong; helping the victim; learning from the experience are all cast aside in favor of the cheapest solution. Most med-mal lawsuits involve both the doctor and the deep-pocket hospital. Generally, the best financial interests of the hospital dictate what is chosen: (A), (B), or (C). The welfare of the injured patient is lost in the game tactics.

Dollars *coming out* of the med-mal system represent a small fraction of the dollars that *go in*. The general rule is that 33% of any trial judgment or settlement goes to the lawyer. Add to this the fact that the majority of injured patients never sue. The result is most of the billions going into the med-mal system never gets to those who need help.

17. Citations 277 and 542 suggest that being completely honest about medical mistakes is the *least* expensive option. Wu (cit. 542) describes our current reality as a malprocess without using the word, writing: "The current system obstructs detection and just compensation for errors and inhibits disclosure."

18. We used systems dynamics to evaluate the medical malpractice system. (cit. 518).

Chapter 4: A System that Thinks

1. "Number 5" refers to the robot hero in the movie *Short Circuit*–well worth your time in contrast to its terrible sequel. In the original movie, a robot soldier comes alive and then refuses to hurt anyone. There are a number of important and not-overwhelming articles and books that help explain systems thinking. Try citations: 2, 4, 15, 39, 235, 254, 255, 326, 327, 412, 469, and 515.

2. Read Stephen Johnson book (cit. 235) titled <u>Emergence</u>. It is fascinating and well worth your time.

3. Surowiecki's book (cit. 480) offers the politically incorrect idea that large groups (crowds) of just average people make better decisions (without central command-and-control) than small groups of experts.

4. You can see how much Lorenz' geometric shape actually does resemble a butterfly's wings at: <u>www.explorations.edu/complexity/java/lorenz.html</u>.

Chapter 5: People and Culture

1. Below are some of the many important healthcare workers you rarely never see.

Technical and Support People in Healthcare	
Technical	**Support/Ancillary**
Radiology: take chest x-rays; do CAT scans	**Human Resources:** Manage the workforce: recruit, train, and retain.
Interventional Radiology: help place medical devices within body, such as for cancer	**Information technology:** install, maintain and upgrade computer systems, and teach users.
Laboratories: do blood counts; measure drug levels, determine the amounts of substances (sodium, potassium, etc.) in the blood.	**Security:** protect security of patients and staff, often in relation to irate or drug-affected family members.
Pharmacy: formulate & distribute medications; advice re: compatibility and adverse impacts.	**Billing**: Manage activities from identifying the billable event through submitting and tracking the bill.

Cardiology: do ECGs & exercise studies	**Risk Management:** Minimize probability of legal complications from hospital activities.
Cardiac Catheterization Lab: assist in diagnostic studies and invasive therapy such as stents and balloon dilation.	**Facilities**: grounds keepers, heat, light, water and power; structural maintenance and contracting; elevators; parking
Ultrasound: do echo studies of head, heart, abdomen, kidneys, blood vessels.	**Chaplain**: Provide spiritual guidance and counseling for those in need.
ER techs: start IV lines; insert tubes; draw blood, move patients. Prepare for suturing. Trained to assist nurses and doctors in crisis situations.	**Transcription**: Responsible for creating permanent, legible accurate records of what was thought, what was done and what happened.
OT & PT techs: prepare materials that occupational and physical therapists use,	**Administration**: The services noted above are all specific. General administration includes most managerial functions such as fiscal services, scheduling, regulatory compliance, and communication with the Board and with Faculty or Medical Staff.
Anesthesia techs: prepare tables with gases, tubing, & other materials for giving anesthesia.	
Neurology techs: prepare and troubleshoot machines used in neurology, such as an EEG.	
OR/scrub/surgical techs: do everything needed to get operating rooms and supplies ready.	
Job descriptions and activities vary by State, institution, organizational structure, and even by culture.	

2. There are a host of articles and books that elucidate organizational and corporate culture. The following citations would be a good starting point: 27, 44, 71, 78, 98, 106, 130, 133, 138, 167, 177, 197, 208, 216, 263, 274, 275, 389, 480, 504, 527, and 547.

3. Maslow, of "Pyramid" fame, was a true rebel. (cit. 320) At the insistence of his parents, he enrolled law school and then immediately dropped out. He defied convention by marrying his first cousin. He stole (do authors say "borrow?") the concept of self-actualization from his colleague, Kurt Goldstein's 1934 book The Organism.

4. *The 100 Best Companies to Work for in America* is citation 293.

5. In his youth, revered American novelist Alistair Maclean had been a fire fighter. Later, he became fascinated by the famous Mann Gulch disaster and memorialized this tragedy in his 1992 book titled *Young Men and Fire* [cit. 310].

6. Carl Weick's article (cit. 527) is highly academic and detailed as well as perceptive and significant.

7. James Champy wrote many useful, interesting books including "Reengineering the Corporation – A Manifesto for Business Revolution." (cit. 91) This book is well worth your time.

8. Our paper (cit. 513) documented the cultural values of hospital CEOs.

9. Harari (cit. 201) also wrote, "Stature within physician society is determined by individual performance rather than teamwork."

10. Dr. Simone was the CEO of a major cancer center who wrote organizational adages (cit. 455) such as: "In academic institutions, muck flows uphill." "In recruiting, first-class people recruit first-class people; second-class people recruit third-class people." "Members of most institutional committees consist of about 30% who will work at it, despite other pressures, and 20% who are idiots, status seekers, or troublemakers."

11. Steiger's report (cit. 468) is worth reading. If you are a doctor, you will see that you are not alone. If you are outside healthcare, note the depression rampant among those at the top of the food chain. This is something only the Public can fix, and should do so in its own best interests.

12. The retention data comes from "The Cost of Turnover" (cit. 507).

13. Congresswoman Nancy Johnson made this prediction in 2001 (cit. 234).

14. Barbara Kellerman (cit. 258) wrote that, "The distinctions among followers are every bit as consequential as those among leaders." She could not be more right.

15. See cit. 508 for a contrast of turnover and retention and cit. 507 for retention data in healthcare workers.

Chapter 6: The Pocket Nerve

1. George Orwell wrote his book *1984* in the year 1948. In his then apocryphal book, he described "newspeak," which was the use of common words but with radically different meanings. For example, in his imagined world of 1984, firemen did not put out fires, they started them in order to burn proscribed books.

2. Our paper on this subject was published in Pediatric Cardiology (cit. 500) with the title, "Physicians must abandon the *illusion* of autonomy for the reality of influence."

3. Regina Herzlinger made that case in her 1997 book titled Market-Driven Health Care (cit. 209).

4. We describe "micro-economic disconnection" in cit. #505 where the consumer and payer are "disconnected."

5. David Goldhill, author and business executive wrote and article in the Atlantic titled "How American Health Care Killed My Father" (http://www.theatlantic.com/doc/print/200909/health-care). While not claiming status as a health care policy expert, he precisely diagnosed what is wrong with healthcare writing that our "system is not worth preserving in anything like its current form and the health-care reform now being contemplated will not fix it."

6. The Report titled "U.S. Health Care: Facts about Cost, Access and Quality" by the Goldman and McGlynn (cit. 180) of the Rand Corporation gives facts rather than opinion or spin.

7. See the *The Globe & Mail*, Saturday July 30, 2005, page A12.

8. Mingardi regales us (cit. 348) with the negative consequences of government control of drug prices.

9. Senator Daschle cited this study in his book, citation 127.

10. In "Market-Driven Healthcare" (cit. 209), Regina Herzlinger provides a raft of information about productivity losses.

11. UMRA = Unfunded Mandates Reform Act; HIPAA = Health Insurance Portability and Accountability Act; CPSIA = Consumer Product Safety Consumer Act. All are Federal laws initially intended to do something helpful that did not have the desired effect and worse had adverse unintended impacts. UMRA showed that Congress ignores Congress. HIPAA did not fix the insurance portability problem and created a costly bureaucracy that creates inefficiency and errors. CPSIA, intended to protect consumers from unsafe products, put hundreds of thousands of small US business people out of business.

12. Citation 541 is a comparison of administrative costs in the USA and Canada. Unfortunately, it underestimates US costs because they did not include regulatory compliance.

13. Kerr's article (cit. 259) is another must-read for everyone, not just those interested in healthcare.

14. See citations 261 and 493.

15. Bryan-Brown "Essay on Criticism" (cit. 79) has much wisdom.

16. See the article at: http://latimes.com/news/local/la-me-medfraud19-2009mar19,0,934741.story reporting on hospital executives who paid kickbacks to people who would recruit homeless persons to pose of sick people in order to fill hospital beds and thus get paid day rates.

17. In just one case (cit. 86) in California, over billing by a medical testing lab resulted in >$100 million in fraudulent charges to Medi-Cal.

Chapter 7: We Get What We Reward

1. Kerr's classic paper (cit. 259) is available on the internet.

2. In their 2005 book _Freakonomics – A Rogue Economist Explores the Hidden Side of Everything_, Steven Levitt and Stephen Gubner (cit. 295) revisited and expanded the concept of perverse incentives as well as the behaviors they induce. The public was so interested in its own perversity that the book became a bestseller.

3. If you want to see doctors demolished–their ethics, abilities, single-mindedness, etc.–just read Shaw's Preface to the Doctor's Dilemma, cit. #440.

4. Behavioral economics describes the rational economic human unit as _homo economicus_ (cit. #359), who seeks always to maximize personal gains. To balance theory with the reality of human behavior, the theorists then say that "homo economicus" has _bounded_ rationality, _bounded_ will power, and _bounded_ self-interest.

5. The following references are but a cursory sampling of the multitude of studies dealing with volume-to-outcome relationships in medicine. See citations: 38, 51, 95, 153, 200, 240, 268, 330, 391, and 456.

6. See our discussion of learning in healthcare in citation 506.

Chapter 8: Cupside Down

1. In his 1999 book, *Ackoff's Best* (cit. 4), the famous management guru describes the differences between data, information, knowledge and wisdom, and how they can and should be used.

2. *The Agenda* is Hammer's sequel to his best-selling *Reengineering the Corporation* (cit. #198).

3. Dee Hock, founder of VISA, wrote an interesting book about how our world is a combination of logic and order with uncertainty (Heisenberg) and chaos. He called our time the Chaordic age in citation 215.

4. There are several different kinds of *bad outcome* in healthcare such as the following.

    *   Adverse effect: something unpleasant or harmful happens to a patient. It may be a complication, an error, even a total surprise.
    *   Avoidable adverse impact: where the cause of the adverse impact is known and adverse impact could have been prevented.
    *   Complication: an adverse impact that can be tied in some way to standard patient care.
    *   Error: being wrong in conduct, judgment or thought. Synonymous with mistake.
    *   Mistake: action or judgment that is misguided or wrong.
    *   Unintended consequence: an outcome that was not intended to result from the treatment.

5. Citation 345 shows what happens when you try a different approach to delivering health care and fail at the outset to build in metrics that show positive as well as negative outcomes.

6. This is another must-read, but you have probably already read it: *Built to Last*, citation 106.

Chapter 9: Practicing Good Medicine

1. The story of Edward R. Morrow is one of heroic commitment to reporting the truth. Morrow actually flew inside British bombers over Germany to get first-hand accurate information to report.

2. Professor Alan Hatch, Emeritus Professor of Communications at University of New Mexico, described these events in a newspaper Opinion piece (cit. 204).

3. See "Psychiatry and the role of the general practitioner" (cit. 539) by Wittkower and Stauble.

4. In the 1980s, we showed that better AND cheaper *were* concurrently possible in healthcare (cit. 498 and 499).

Chapter 10: Reprising Jerry Maguire

1. An article by Dr. K Sheikh (cit. 442) dramatizes *perfection paralysis*. Analyzing 128 studies of the volume-to-outcome relationship in surgery, Sheikh reported that only 103 showed a statistically significant reduction in mortality with volume of patients. *Only* 81% (103/128) showed a relationship. Because it was less than 100%, Sheikh demanded that no action be taken without prospective, double blind studies. Perfectly controlled research studies may be possible with test tubes and in rats but are impossible or unethical in humans. If doctors had waited for perfect data, we would have no antibiotics, anesthesia or transplants.

2. In his seminal 1994 article titled *Error in Medicine* (cit. 290), Dr. Lucian Leape described how the "name, blame, and shame" handling of medical errors actually reinforced having more errors in the future.

3. A song in the Rock Hudson-Doris Day movie *Pajama Game* is titled, "I am a time study man." Such time-motion studies were made famous (?infamous) by Frederic Taylor. Sadly, the lyrics of the song still dominate management thinking just as they did in 1954 when the movie aired. The concept of humans as machine parts should have been retired half a century ago.

4. Baptist System in Memphis was one of the first healthcare systems to win the Baldrige Award. The system CEO, Al Stubblefield, shared their road to glory in citation 477.

5. Though George Bernard Shaw is thought to have originated "The road to hell is paved with good intentions," credit belongs to Boswell quoting Samuel Jackson on April 16, 1775: "Hell is paved with good intentions."

6. Blumenthal and his colleagues (cit. 58) described what happened when China dismantled their safety net of bare-foot doctors and did not replace it.

7. Even if you do not like science fiction, Robert Heinlein's book "The Moon is a harsh mistress" is simply a must-read. I guarantee that you will enjoy it…and it will make you think.

8. In cit. #301 Floyd Loop wrote, "The enemy of every hospital is its own infrastructure." He was spot on. Most hospitals do not recognize that the most important component of their infrastructure is their people.

9. I refer to Russ Ackoff's books because there is so much wisdom contained therein. Just like Heinlein's "Moon is a harsh mistress," "Ackoff's Best" (cit. #4) is a must-read.

10. Citations #54 and #363 describe application of Baldrige principles to healthcare and health care.

11. "And then there was One" in *Birth of the Chaordic Age*, citation 215.

12. Some people find a mantra to be helpful. I offer *Stop3–Start3* below.
    Stop#1: Blaming
    It is our natural, very human tendency to blame someone when the lights go out, when we have a complication after surgery, or when our job gets downsized. Blaming the system is not satisfying. The system does not have a face you can stick your tongue out at or a body you can throw rocks at. We

need to *stop assigning blame* – for two reasons. First, most bad outcomes are system issues rather than individual problems, but much more important, blaming never fixes anything. We may feel better but the problem remains unresolved.

Stop#2: Confusing

We are all guilty of treating the obvious symptoms, the blatant signs of problems in our everyday lives. Light goes out? Change the light bulb. Have a bad medical outcome? It must be the doctor's fault. Lose your job? Just LOOK at the CEO's obscene bonus!

Medical errors; millions without insurance; avoidable deaths during health care; nursing shortages: these are all symptoms, not causes. Treating these symptoms will never cure the patient called healthcare. We need to *stop confusing symptoms with causes.*

Stop#3: Wishing

We live in a world of sound bytes. We all want, need, and frankly expect the simple, quick and easy answer. If our wishful thinking were not bad enough, we look to the person with a fancy title to provide the silver bullet that makes everything come out right.

Patient's Bill of Rights. Single payer system. Universal health care. These are nice catch phrases and election year slogans but not real solutions. The Lone Ranger may have silver bullets and Harry Potter has magic potions, but in our world, simple, quick answers to complex, long-standing problems do not exist. We need to *stop magical thinking.* Wishing will not make it so.

Start#1: Believing

Our hardest job is to change ourselves. As long as we are part of the "consensus of futility," nothing will improve. Because we *know* healthcare cannot be fixed, we do not try. Because we do not try, it stays the same. This is a classic self-fulfilling prophecy. Only we can break this cycle. If we want better and cheaper health care, then *start believing that we can* have both.

Start#2: Identifying

To fix anything, we must treat the reasons for dysfunction. This means we must first start to *identify the true causes.* In healthcare, WHY are millions without insurance? Treat that why. WHY are there avoidable medical errors and deaths? Make these underlying reasons go away. WHY are healthcare costs constantly rising? Figure this out, deal with the WHY, and healthcare costs will fall. (Without Start #1, numbers 2 and 3 will not happen.)

Start#3: Communicating

We need to accept that only we and only we – the general Public – have the need and the power to fix healthcare. There is too much inertia and far too many special interests to expect the government to solve our problem. We have to start the change process ourselves. This will begin when we *start communicating with each other* about what is really wrong with healthcare and what we really want. After we agree on causes, then we can discuss what we are going to do about them. When we have consensus on our desired outcomes, we can begin to achieve them.

Chapter 11: Uproot!

1. Machiavelli's book "The Prince" (cit. #308) described all morals issues exclusively in terms of effect on political gain: acceptable, cruel but effective, or useless.

2. I dated the start of modern medicine with the first surgery under anesthesia. Harvard's lecture on the History of Anesthesia is given in the famous Ether Dome, where the first surgical patient was operated under open drop ether to put him to sleep. The tiered benches are the same incredibly uncomfortable wooden ones that the doctors sat on in 1848.

3. Regina Herzlinger is quoted from citation 209. Business leaders such as Lee Scott, former CEO of Wal-Mart, have echoed similar sentiments in highly public forums.

4. Former Senator Tom Daschle wrote a book titled "Critical" [cit. #127] in which he proposed solving healthcare by the creation of a governing body, the FHB (Federal Health Board) that would effectively control all elements of the system. Mr. Daschle was proposed by newly installed President Obama as the Director of Health and Human Services but Mr. Daschle withdrew before his nomination hearings.

5. For a projection of what government-controlled healthcare such as Great Britain's NHS might look like here, read Daniel Putkowski's fictional account titled "Universal Coverage" (Hawser Press 2009). There are numerous reports of how bad things can get in other countries' "universal" healthcare systems on the Internet. One example can be found at: http://hotair.com/archives/2010/01/vip-treatment-under-nationalized-health-care.

6. Stephen Spear showed how the Toyota system worked as a learning organization (cit. #465) and later suggested application of Toyota principles as an answer to our healthcare woes (Cit. #466).

7. Dr. David Brailer was tasked by President GW Bush to "fix healthcare" (cit# 360). He recommended implementing a national health information system...and lasted less than a year in his job.

8. The title of David Dilts' paper (cit. #140) sounds highly specialty-specific but the message is widely applicable and highly important for anyone who plans, performs, or administers research of any kind, not just biomedical. His flow chart is shown on the next page.

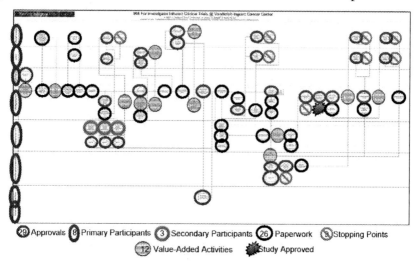

29 Approvals 8 Primary Participants 3 Secondary Participants 26 Paperwork Stopping Points
12 Value-Added Activities Study Approved

9. Doctors resist standardization at both conscious and subconscious levels. They think *people are not machine parts on an assembly line,* and *if each person is unique, so should be their medical care.* Doctors are socialized to have personal responsibility and not give it up to some procedure manual. To their credit, nurses are much more comfortable with systematized approaches and clinical pathways. They utilize policies, procedures, and checklists. Patients want to be special, unique individuals, not *the belly pain in room 315.* The regulatory system believes that it should protect by standardization, not the providers, and that their regulatory compliance protocols provide that protection. Read how this played out in http://www.fiercehealthcare.com/story/hhs-oks-mi-infection-checklists/2008-02-20.

10. Anyone interested in medical information technology should read Walker's paper (cit #519.)

11. Over 80% of new medical drugs or devices approved by the FDA come from the USA. The medical systems of other countries depend on the USA for the latest technologies to combat disease.

12. Kurt Lewin 1947 work (cit. # 296) described how all change is a balance of drivers and resistors, and that you get more *bang for your buck* by reducing resistance than by increasing the drive.

13. Stephen Covey's book "The Seven Habits of Highly Effective People" (cit. #119).

Chapter 12: A healthy tree

1. JD Klienke's book <u>Bleeding Edge</u> (cit. 262) is a rant worth reading.

2. Fred Friendly was the President of News at CBS TV. He resigned in 1966 when senior management ran an episode of *I Love Lucy* in place of what he had scheduled: the first U.S. Senate debate over American involvement in Vietnam. Friendly joined the Ford Foundation where he formulated the *Ethics in America* series. If you ever get a chance to view them, do so. In the movie *Good Night, and Good luck* (about Edward R. Murrow), George Clooney played the part of Fred Friendly.

3. Dr. Henry Simmons was quoted by columnist Dan Broder in 2002 (cit. 74).

4. Schumpeter's concept of creative destruction (http://en.wikipedia.org/wiki/Creative_destruction.) is as applicable to healthcare as it is to economics.

5. Dr. Elisabeth Kübler-Ross (1926-2004) opened the topic of Death and Dying – the title of her 1969 book – to frank discussion. She made it possible to talk openly about the final phase of life.

6. We discuss the GAP between managers and providers in detail in citations #513 & #516. The most surprising aspect of the studies was the commonality of core values.

About the Author

There is one sure thing: you either need health care now or will in the future. The system we currently have doesn't work, will not be there for you, and needs to be fixed. Lots of people tell you how to fix it or to be more accurate, how *they* will fix it. Deane has a totally different approach. Why should you listen to him?

Background facts on the author include the following. Schooling and training at: Yale, Chicago Medical School, Mayo Clinic, Northwestern, Harvard, and Anderson Management Schools. Deane has authored over 100 academic publications as well as numerous lay articles and blogs on both the practice of medicine and healthcare strategy. He has been Chief of Section at San Diego Children's, University of Chicago and University of New Mexico, as well as a pediatric cardiologist for over 35 years.

Deane's past–both professional and personal–has exposed him to every aspect of healthcare and health care: practicing medicine, administration, research, teaching, as well as being a critically ill patient himself. Combining those experiences with his MBA knowledge along with his research in management and business, Deane shares insights into the root causes of why the healthcare system continues to fail patients, nurses, doctors, and our country, and most important, *what you can do about it*.

Democrats, Republicans and I all claim we are working in the best interests of the American people. The difference between them and me is simple. I have nothing to gain. After reading this book, you decide whose approach will cure U.S. healthcare.

An Alternative To Med-Mal: The Office of Medical Injuries (OMIn)

Since the problem is the system itself, treatment must be focused on the system rather than the individuals. If, as has been shown, the problem is system design rather than implementation, then "dissolving" dysfunction requires a new system. Such a system is proposed below, called the OMIn.

A functional system such as an OMIn will accomplish two socially desirable goals: (1) Help those injured in relation to their health care; and (2) Provide for (encourage) continuous quality improvement, which includes but is not limited to error-reduction.

The OMIn will require enabling legislation, including creation of a secure national medical database. The current med-mal system will not be officially dismantled but patients will be offered *either* the current tort system *or* application to the OMIn but not both.

The OMIn will have four Divisions: Compensation; Dissolution; Improvements; and Oversight. Evidence reported to or collected by OMI will be exempt from the legal process, that is, it will not be admissible in Court.

Compensation Division

Any medical injury can be reported by the injured patient, a family member, or an involved medical professional. The Compensation Section, staffed with medical experts and actuaries, will evaluate the facts of the injury, determine the severity and time of dysfunction related to the injury and offer appropriate compensation. The Compensation Division can request additional medical information even tests in order to make its determinations. This Division will also accept testimonial and other evidence submitted by the family or patient.

The patient can, at his or her choosing, offer a different calculation for compensation based on advice from experts retained by the injured party at his/her expense. The Compensation Division will review the additional data and analysis. If it deems necessary, the Division will amend the proposed compensation scheme.

Within 90 days of completion of its analysis, the Compensation Division will pass on the case file with all the facts to both the Dissolution Division and the Oversight Division (see below).

Dissolution Division

To "dissolve" a problem means to change the system so that the problem can never recur. The Dissolution Division is tasked with learning from the experience involved in the injury. The Division will work in concert with the involved local professionals and the Healthcare Institution where the injury occurred to determine how and why the injury occurred and if possible, to design a way to prevent the injury from ever happening again.

159

The Dissolution Division will be staffed with consulting experts in both medical and management areas, from subspecialties such as Cardiology and Endocrinology to Operations, Organizational Behavior, and Technologic Innovation.

Sometimes the cause of an injury cannot be determined. In such cases, a dissolving recommendation may not be possible. In most cases, a way can be devised to prevent recurrence. The Dissolution Division will not only help develop such an improvement but monitor the implementation of the change in the Institution or system where the injury occurred.

The Dissolution Division is required to pass on its findings to the Improvement Division within 90 days of completion of study and design of change. It is not required to wait until the change has been implemented and tested.

Improvements Division

The Improvements Division will be staffed in a similar manner to the Dissolution Division with consultants in both medical and management areas, from subspecialties such as Cardiology and Endocrinology to Operations, Organizational Behavior, and Technologic Innovation.

The Improvements Division receives all the findings and specific recommendations from the Dissolution Division. It collates and analyzes this data looking for trends and for improvements that can be generalized: improvements that would work in many facilities rather than just the one where the original injury occurred. When such improvements are found, they are distributed to all US healthcare facilities by online distribution as well as to the Oversight Division. The Improvements Division is not tasked with overseeing the implementation of such recommended improvements. It is required only to distribute the information. Implementation is left to the discretion of each healthcare system or institution.

Oversight Division

All case files as well as all recommended improvements are shared with the Oversight Division, which looks for patterns of recurring medical injuries after the wide distribution of a Dissolution Recommendation specific to that injury. Either the recommendation does not work (and the injuries recur) or institutions are being negligent. The Division, staffed primarily with experts in medicine, is tasked with determining trends and differentiating (A) recommendation failure from (B) institution failure. When the Division decides it is (A), the Oversight Division confers with the Improvements Division to modify the Recommendation and then distribute the revision. When the determination is (B), the case is referred to appropriate disciplinary services, be it medical society, professional organization or an accreditation body such as JCAHO.

Financing the OMIn

As everyone benefits from the OMIn, everyone should pay for the OMIn. Like social security, there will be a large time lag between a person's payment into the OMIn and need for compensation to that individual injured patient. Of course, it is hoped that like all catastrophic insurance, the individual will never need the OMIn, but we know many will.

It is presently impossible to predict accurately how much the OMIn will cost but a reasonable upper limit would be $20 billion per year. This is less than any current estimate of the cost of defensive medicine alone and a small fraction of the current cost of medical liability insurance as well as legal costs, all of which will disappear as the OMIn replaces the med-mal system. Net savings to the nation will exceed $100 billion per year.

A new tax will be added to what is now the social security tax, called OMIn tax. This money will be sequestered from the General Fund and accounted separately so that the actual expenses of OMI can be easily determined and the OMI tax adjusted in subsequent years.

Articles by "Waldman, JD" that are completely underlined are available for immediate reading by download from www.uproothealthcare.com.

1. Ackoff RL, Emery FE. 1972. On Purposeful Systems. Chicago: Aldine-Atherton.

2. Ackoff RL. 1978. The Art of Problem Solving, Accompanied by Ackoff's Fables. Wiley & Sons, New York.

3. Ackoff RL. 1989. From Data to Wisdom. *Journal of Applied Systems Analysis* 16: 3-9.

4. Ackoff RL. 1999. Ackoff's Best-His Classic Writings on Management. Wiley & Sons, New York.

5. Ackoff RL, Rovin S. 2003. Redesigning Society. Stanford Business Books: Stanford, C

6. Aiken LH, Clarke SP, Sloane DM, Sochalski J, Silber JH. October 23/30, 2002. Hospital Nurse Staffing and Patient Mortality, Nurse Burnout, and Job Dissatisfaction. *Journal of American Medical Association* 286(16): 1987-1993

7. Alexander JA, Fennell M. 1986. Patterns of decision making in multihospital systems. *Journal of Health and Social Behavior* 27(1): 14-27.

8. Alexander JA, Lichtenstein R, Oh H, Ullman E. 1998. A causal model of voluntary turnover among nursing personnel in long-term psychiatric settings. *Research in Nursing and Health* 21(5): 415-427.

9. Allen SW, Gauvreau K, Bloom BT, Jenkins KJ. 2003. Evidence-based referral results in significantly reduced mortality after congenital heart surgery. *Pediatrics* 112(1): 24-28.

10. Anderson GF, Hussey PS, Frogner BK, Waters HR. 2005. Health spending in the United States and the rest of the industrialized world. *Health Affairs* 24(4): 903-914.

11. Angell M. October 13, 2002. The forgotten domestic crisis. *New York Times,* Op-Ed,

12. Anonymous. March/April 2003. Research Notes. *Healthcare Executive* 18(2): 42.

13. Anonymous. Jul/Aug 2004. Hospital CEO turnover remains stable in 2003. *Healthcare Executive* 19(4): 65.

14. Argote L, Epple D. Learning Curves in Manufacturing. *Science* February 1990; 247: 920–24.

15. Aronson D. 1996-98. Overview of Systems Thinking. www.thinking.net. Accessed Feb 2004.

16. Arndt M, Bigelow B. 2000. The transfer of business practices into hospitals: history and implications. *Advances in Health Care Management* Vol. 1: 339-368.

17. Ashkanasy NM, Broadfoot LE, Falkus S. 2000. Questionnaire measures of organizational culture. In Neal M. Ashkanazy, Celeste P. M. Wilderon, and Mark F. Peterson (Eds.), Handbook of organizational culture and climate (pp. 131-145). Thousand Oaks, CA: Sage Publications

18. Ashmos DP, McDaniel RR. 1991. Physician participation in hospital strategic decision making: The effect of hospital strategy and decision content. *Health Services Research* 26(3): 375-401.

References

19. Ashmos DP, McDaniel RR. 1996. Understanding the participation of critical task specialists in strategic decision making. *Decision Science* Winter 27(1): 103-121.

20. Ashmos DP, Duchon D, McDaniel RR. 1998. Participation in strategic decision making: The role of organizational predisposition and issue interpretation. *Decision Sciences* 29(1): 25-51.

21. Ashmos DP, Huonker JW, McDaniel RR. 1998. The effect of clinical professional and middle manager participation on hospital performance. *Health Care Management Review* 23(4): 7-20.

22. Ashmos DP, Duchon D, McDaniel RR. 2000. Organizational response to complexity: the effect on organizational performance. *Journal of Organizational Change* 13(6): 577-594.

23. Associated Press, April 4, 2007. "Doctor contrasts his cancer care with uninsured patient who died." Accessed March 2009 at: www.cnn.com/2007/HEALTH/04/04/uninsured.dead.ap/index.html.

24. Associated Press. April 18, 2007. Researchers: Let's Scrap the Internet and Start Over. Accessed May 14, 2007 at: www.foxnews.com/story/0,2933,266124,00.html.

25. Atwater JB, Pittman PH. 2006. Facilitating systemic thinking in business classes. *Decision Sciences Journal of Innovative Education* July, 4(2): 273-292.

26. Axelsson R. 1998. Toward an evidence-based health care management. *International Journal of health Planning and Management* 13; 307-17

27. Baker E. 2001. Learning from the Bristol Inquiry. *Cardiology in the Young* 11: 585-587.

28. Baker T. 1999. Doing Well by Doing Good, Economic Policy Institute, Washington, DC.

29. Baloff, N. 1971. Extension of the Learning Curve—Some Empirical Results. *Operational Research Quarterly* 1971; 22(4): 329–40.

30. Barnard A, Tong K. 2000. The doctor is out. *Boston Globe*, July 9: A18.

31. Barzansky B, Etzel SI. September 5, 2001. Educational programs in the US medical schools 2000-2001. *Journal of American Medical Association* 286(9): 1049-1055

32. Bass CD. 2000. Medicine losing its workhorses. *Albuquerque Journal*, September 17, 2000; page I-2.

33. Barrett R. January 27, 2002. The Apprentices--Construction trades need more people willing to learn while they earn. Albuquerque Journal I-1 & 2.

34. Barron JM, McCafferty S. September 1977. Job search, labor supply, and the quit decision: Theory and evidence. *American Economic Review* 67(4): 683-691.

35. Bartol KM. December 1979. Professionalism as a predictor of organizational commitment, role stress, and turnover: A multidimensional approach. *Academy of Management Journal* 22(4): 815-821.

36. Becker T. 2004. Why pragmatism is not practical. *Journal of Management Inquiry September* 13(3): 224-230. See Jacobs (2004) for companion article.

37.   Beedham T. 1996. Why do young doctors leave medicine? *British Journal of Hospital Medicine* 55(11): 699-701 with Editorial Comments by Elizabeth Paice 1997; 90(8): 417-418 and by John Davis 1997; 90(10): 585.

38.   Begg CB, Cramer LD, Hoskins WJ, Brennan MF. 1998. Impact of Hospital Volume on Operative Mortality for Cancer Surgery. *Journal of the American Medical Association* 280: 1747–51.

39.   Beinhocker, ED. 1997. Strategy at the edge of chaos. *The McKinsey Quarterly* Winter #1, pp. 24-40.

40.   Beller GA. 2000. Academic Health Centers: The making of a crisis and potential remedies. *J Amer Coll Cardiol* 36:1428-31

41.   Bender C, DeVogel S, Blomberg R. 1999. The socialization of newly hired medical staff into a large health system. *Health Care Management Review* 24:95-108.

42.   Berenson RA Ginsburg PB, May JH. 2007. Hospital-physician relations: Cooperation, competition, or separation? *Health Affairs* 26(1): w31-w43

43.   Berger JE, Boyle RL. November/December 1992. How to avoid the high costs of physician turnover. *MGM Journal* pp. 80-91.

44.   Berry LL. 2004. The Collaborative Organization: Leadership lessons from Mayo Clinic. *Organizational Dynamics* 33(3): 228-242.

45.   Berta WB, Baker R. 2004. Factors that impact the transfer and retention of best practices for reducing error in hospital. *Health Care Management Review* 29(2): 90-97.

46.   (von) Bertalanffy L. 1968. General System theory: Foundation, development, applications. George Braziller, New York, revised edition 1976.

47.   Berwick DM. 1989. Continuous Improvement as an ideal in health care. *New England Journal of Medicine* 320(1): 53-56.

48.   Berwick DM, Godfrey AB, Roessner J. 1990. Curing Health Care. Jossey-Bass, San Francisco, CA.

49.   Bettis RW, Prahahald CK. 1995. The dominant logic: retrospective and extension. *Strategic Management Journal* 16(1): 237-252.

50.   Beyer JM and Trice HM: "Using Six Organizational Rites to Change Culture" pages 370-399. In: Kilmann RH, Saxton MJ, Serpa R, et al (1985) Gaining Control of the Corporate Culture. San Franciso: Jossey-Bass.

51.   Birkmeyer JD, Finlayson SR, Tosteson AN, Sharp SM, Warshaw AL, Fisher ES. 1999. "Effect of Hospital Volume on In-hospital Mortality with Pancreaticoduodenectomy." *Surgery* 125: 250–56

52.   Birkmeyer JD, Stukel TA, Siewers AE, et al. 2003. Surgeon volume and operative mortality in the United States. *New England Journal of Medicine* 349: 2117-27.

53.   Bisognano M. 2004. What Juran says. One of four essays on "Can the gurus' concepts cure healthcare?" In *Quality Progress* September pp. 33-34.

54.   Blackburn R, Rosen B. 1993. Total quality and human resource management: lessons learned from Baldrige award-winning companies. *Academy of Management Executive* 7: 49-66.

55. Blaufuss J, Maynard J, Schollars G. 1992a. Calculating and Updating Nursing Turnover Costs. *Nursing Economic$* January/February 10(1): 39-45, 78.

56. Blaufuss J, Maynard J, Schollars G. 1992b. Methods of evaluating turnover costs. *Nursing Management* 23(5): 52-59.

57. Bloom J, Alexander JA, Nuchols B. 1992. The effect of the social organization of work on the voluntary turnover rate of hospital nurses in the United States. *Social Science and Medicine* 34(12): 1413-1424.

58. Blumenthal D, Hsiao. September 15, 2005. Privatization and Its Discontents-The Evolving Chinese Health Care System. *The New England Journal of Medicine* 353: 1165-1170.

59. Bolster CJ, Hawthorne G, Schubert P. Nov/Dec 2002. "Executive compensation survey: Can money buy happiness?" *Trustee* 55(10): 8-12.

60. Bonacich, P. 1987. Power and Centrality: A Family of Measures. *American Journal of Sociology* 92(5): 1170-82.

61. Borda RG, Norman IJ. 1997. Factors influencing turnover and absence of nurses: a research review. *International Journal of Nursing Studies* 34(6): 385-394.

62. Bowles S, Gintis H. 1998. The Evolution of Strong Reciprocity. Santa Fe Institute Working Paper, SFI 98-08-073E. Accessed on January 14, 2007 at: http://citeseer.ist.psu.edu/bowles98evolution.html.

63. Bradbury, R. 1966. Farenheit 451. Sundance Books, Littleton, MA. Reprinted 2002.

64. Bragg JE, Andrews IR. 1973. Participative decision-making: An experimental study in a hospital. *Journal of Applied Behavioral Science* 9: 727-735.

65. Brass DJ. 1984. Being in the right place: A structural analysis of individual influence in an organization. *Administrative Science Quarterly*, 29: 518-539.

66. Brass DJ, Burkhardt ME. 1993. Potential power and power use: An investigation of structure and behavior. *Academy of Management Journal* 36(3): 441-470.

67. Brennan TA, Localio AR, Leape LL, et al. 1990. Identification of Adverse Effects Occurring during Hospitalization: A Cross-Sectional Study of Litigation, Quality Assurance, and Medical Records at Two Teaching Hospitals. *Ann Int Med* 112: 221-226.

68. Brennan TA, Sox CM, Burstin HR. 1996. Relation Between Negligent Adverse Events and the Outcomes of Medical-Malpractice Litigation. *N Engl J Med* 335:1963-1967.

69. Brewer LA, Fosburg RG, Mulder GA, Verska JJ (1972) Spinal cord complications following surgery for coarctation of the aorta. *J Thorac Cardiovasc Surg* 64(3): 368-381

70. Brook RH, Lohr KN (1987) Monitoring quality of care in the Medicare Program. *JAMA* 258: 3138-3141.

71. Bristol Royal Infirmary Inquiry Final Report, July 2001; Accessed March 15, 2006 at: www.bristol-inquiry.org.uk/final_report/index.htm.

72. Brockschmidt, FR. 1996. Corporate culture: does it play a role in health care management? *CRNA* 1994; 5:93-6.

73. Broder DS. October 21, 2001. Need for capable government has never been clearer. *Albuquerque Journal,* B2

74. Broder DS. April 17, 2002. Health cost spike can't be ignored. *Albuquerque Journal,* A12

75. Broder DS. March 18, 2005. Unfunded mandates still plaguing states, cities. Albuquerque Journal, #77, A14.

76. Brooks I. 1996. Using rituals to reduce barriers between sub-cultures. *J Mgmt Med* 10(3): 23-30.

77. Brotherton SE, Simon FA, Etzel SI (September 5, 2001) US Graduate medical education 2000-2001. *Journal of American Medical Association* 286(9): 1056-1060.

78. Bruner EM, Ed. 1983. Text, play, and story: the construction and reconstruction of self and society: 1983 Proceedings of the American Ethnological Society. Waveland Press; Prospect Heights, Ill, 1988.

79. Bryan-Brown C, Dracup K. 2001. An Essay on Criticism. *American Journal of Critical Care* 10(1): 1-4

80. Bryson RW, Aderman M, Sampiere JM, Rockmore L, Matsuda T. 1985. Intensive care nurse: Job tension and satisfaction as a function of experience level. *Critical Care Medicine* 13(9): 767-769.

81. Buchan J, Seccombe I. June 13, 1991. The high cost of turnover. *Health Services Journal* 101(5256): 27-28.

82. Buckbinder SB, Wilson M, Melick CF, Powe NR. 2001. Primary care physician job satisfaction and turnover. *American Journal of Managed Care* 7(7): 701-713.

83. Buckingham M, Coffman C. 1999. First, Break All The Rules. Simon and Schuster: New York

84. Burne J. April 16, 2005. Cleaning up MRSA. *The [London] Times,* A12.

85. Burt RS, MJ Miner MJ (eds.) 1983. Applied Network Analysis: A Methodological Introduction. Beverly Hills: Sage.

86. California Healthline, March 20, 2009. "Suit Says Lab Firms Overbilled Medi-Cal for Testing Services." Accessed April 2009 at: http://www.californiahealthline.org/Articles/2009/3/20/Suit-Says-Lab-Firms-Overbilled-MediCal-for-Testing-Services.aspx.

87. Cameron KS, Freeman SJ. 1991. Cultural congruence, Strength, and Type: Relationships to Effectiveness. *Research in Organizational Change and Development* 5: 23-58.

88. Carroll L. Reprinted in 1994. Alice in Wonderland and Through the Looking-Glass. Quality Paperback Book Club: New York.

89. Carvel J. November 23, 2005. NHS cash crisis bars knee and hip replacements for obese. *Manchester Guardian,* Page 1

90. Cavanaugh SJ. 1990. Predictors of Nursing staff turnover. *Journal of Advanced Nursing* 15(3): 373-380.

91. Champy J. 1995. Reengineering Management. HarperBusiness: New York.
92. Charles SC, Gibbons RD, Frisch PR, Pyskoty CE, Hedeker D, Singha NK. 1992. Predicting Risk for Medical Malpractice Claims Using Quality-of-Care Characteristics. *Western Journal of Medicine* 157:433-439.
93. Chassin MR. 1998. Is health care ready for six sigma quality? *The Millbank Quarterly* Winter v76 i4 p 565(2)
94. Christenson CM, Bohmer R, Kenagy J. 2000. Will disruptive innovations cure health care? *Harvard Business Review* 78(5): 102-112.
95. Clark RE. 1996. Outcome as a Function of Annual Coronary Artery Bypass Graft Volume. *Annals of Thoracic Surgery* 6(1): 21–26.
96. Claybrook J. 2004. Don't blame lawsuits for rising malpractice insurance rates. *USA Today* Tuesday January 27; p. 19A.
97. Cochrane AL. 1972. Effectiveness and Efficiency: Random Reflections of Health Services. London: Nuffield Trust.
98. Coeling HVE, Wilcox JR. 1988. Understanding organizational culture: A key to management decision-making. *J of Nursing Admin* 18(11): 16-24.
99. Coeling HVE, Simms LM (1993) "Facilitating Innovations at the Nursing Unit Level through Cultural Assessment, Part 1: How to keep Management Ideas from Falling on Deaf Ears." *Journal of Nursing Administration* 23: 46-53.
100. Coeling HVE, Simms LM. 1993. Facilitating Innovation at the unit level through cultural assessment, Part 2. *J of Nursing Admin* 23(5): 13-20.
101. Cohn KH, Peetz ME. 2003. Surgeon frustration: Contemporary problems, practical solutions. *Contemporary Surgery*. 59(2): 76-85.
102. Cohn KH, Gill S, Schwartz R. 2005. Gaining hospital administrators' attention: Ways to improve physician-hospital management dialogue. *Surgery* 137:132-140
103. Cohn KH. 2005. Embracing Complexity, from Cohn KH. *Better Communication for Better Care: Mastering Physician-Administrator Collaboration*, Chicago, Health Administration Press, Pp. 30-38.
104. Coile RC. 1994. "Movement toward managed care leads to shifts in organizational cultures." *Georgia Hospitals Today* 38:4-6.
105. Coleman J, Katz E, Menzel. December 1957. "The diffusion of an innovation among physicians." *Sociometry* 20(4): 253-270.
106. Collins JC, Porras JI. 1997. Built to Last. HarperBusiness: New York.
107. Collins J. 2001. Good to Great. HarperBusiness, New York.
108. Command Paper: CM 5207. July 2001. The Inquiry into the management of care of children receiving complex heart surgery at the Bristol Royal Infirmary – Final Report. Accessed March 2006 at: www.bristol-inquiry.org.uk.
109. Conger JA, Kanungo RN. 1988. The empowerment process: Integrating theory and practice. *Academy of Management Review* 13: 471-482.
110. Conlin M. Smashing the Clock. YahooBusinessOnLine accessed December 8, 2006 at: http://biz.yahoo.com/special/allbiz120606_article1.html.

111. Connelly LM, Bott M, Hoffart N, Taunton RL. 1997. Methodologic triangulation in a study of nurse retention. *Nursing Research* Sept/Oct 46(5): 299-302

112. Conner D. 1990. Corporate culture: Healthcare's change master. *Healthcare Executive* 5: 28-9.

113. Consumer Reports February 2007. "Get better care from your doctor." Accessed January 4, 2006 at: www.ConsumerReports

114. Cooke R, Szumal J. 1991. Measuring normative beliefs and shared behavioral expectations in organizations: The Reliability and Validity of the Organizational Culture Inventory. *Psychological Reports* 72: 1299-1330.

115. Cooke RA, Szumal J. 2000. Using the organizational culture inventory to understand operating cultures of organizations. In Neal M. Ashkanasy, Celeste P. M. Wilderon, and Mark F. Peterson (Eds.), *Handbook of organizational culture and climate* (pp. 147-162). Thousand Oaks, CA: Sage Publications.

116. Cotton JL, Vollrath DA, Froggatt KL, Lengnick-Hall ML, Jennings KR. 1988. Employee participation: Diverse forms and different outcomes. *Academy of Management Review*, 13(1): 8-22.

117. Coulson JD, Seddon MR, Readdy WF. March 2008. Advancing Safety in pediatric cardiology – Approaches Developed in Aviation. *Congenital Cardiology Today*, Vol 6, No. 3, Pp 1-10.

118. Coutu DL. 2002. The anxiety of Learning. [Interview with Edgar Schein]. *Harvard Business Review* March, pp 100-106.

119. Covey, SR 1989. The Seven Habits Of Highly Effective People. Simon & Schuster: New York.

120. Cuny J (2005) "Failure to Rescue–2004 Benchmarking Project." Accessed June 2005 at: www.uhc.edu.

121. Cutler DM, Rosen AB, Vijan S. 2006. The Value of Medical Spending in the United States, 1960-2000. *The New England Journal of Medicine* 355(9): 920-927.

122. D'Aunno T, Alexander JA, Laughlin C. 1996. Business as usual? Changes in Health Care's workforce and organization of work. *Hospital and Health Services Administration* 16: 3-18.

123. Dalton DR, Todor WD. 1979. Turnover turned over: An expanded and positive perspective. Acade*my of Management Review* 4: 225-35.

124. Damasio AR. 1994. Descartes' Error: Emotion, Reason and the Human Brain. Avon Books: New York.

125. Danzon PM. 1985. *Medical Malpractice: Theory, Evidence and Public Policy.* Harvard University Press, Cambridge, MA.

126. Danzon PM. 1986. New evidence on the frequency and severity of medical malpractice claims. Rand Corporation, Santa Monica, CA. R-3410-ICJ.

127. Daschle, T Greenberger, SS, Lambrew JM. 2008. Critical: What We Can Do About the Health-Care Crisis. New York: St. Martin's Press.

128. Davidson M. 1983. <u>Uncommon Sense – The Life and Thought of Ludwig von Bertalanffy (1901-1972), Father of General Systems Theory</u>. Tarcher, Inc., Los Angeles.

129. Dauten D. 2001. The cost of being ordinary. <u>Dale@dauten.com</u>

130. Davies HTO, Nutley SM, Mannion R. 2000. Organizational Culture and Quality of Health Care. *Quality in Health Care* 9: 111-9.

131. Davis TRV: "Managing Culture at the Bottom" pages 163-182. In: Kilmann RH, Saxton MJ, Serpa R, et al (1985) <u>Gaining Control of the Corporate Culture</u>. San Franciso: Jossey-Bass.

132. Davis SM: "Culture Is Not Just and Internal Affair" pages 137-147. In: Kilmann RH, Saxton MJ, Serpa R, et al (1985) <u>Gaining Control of the Corporate Culture</u>. San Franciso: Jossey-Bass.

133. Deal TE, Kennedy AA. 1982. <u>Corporate Culture: Rites and Rituals of Corporate Life</u>. Perseus Publishing, Cambridge, MA.

134. Deal TE: "Cultural Change: Opportunity, Silent Killer, or Metamorphosis?" pages 292-331. In: Kilmann RH, Saxton MJ, Serpa R, et al (1985) <u>Gaining Control of the Corporate Culture</u>. San Franciso: Jossey-Bass.

135. Deal TE, Kennedy AA. 1999. <u>The New Corporate Cultures.</u> Perseus Books, Reading MA.

136. Deems RS. 1999. Calculating the true cost of employee turnover. *Balance* 3(3): 13

137. Degeling P, Kennedy J, Hill, M. 1998. Do Professional Subcultures Set the Limits of Hospital Reform? *Clinician in Management* 7: 89-98.

138. Denison DR, Spreitzer GM. 1991. Organizational culture and organizational development: a competing values approach, *Research in Organizational Change and Development*, 5:1-21.

139. Desjardins RE. 1997. Does your corporate culture contribute to the problem? *Food & Drug Law Journal* 52:169-71.

140. Dilts DM, Sandler AB. 2006. The "Invisible" Barriers to Clinical Trials: The impact of Structural, Infrastructural, and Procedural Barriers to Opening Oncology Clinical Trials," *Journal Clinical Oncology*, 24(28): 4545-52.

141. Dixon K. 2004. "HMOs bringing back unpopular cost controls-Survey." Reuters, 8/10/04. Accessed 8/10/04 at: http//:news.yahoo.com/news?tmpl=story&cid=571&u= /nm/20040811/hl_nm/health_hmos_study.

142. Dobyns L. March 20, 2006. "How hospitals heal themselves." At: <u>www.managementwisdom.com/goodnews.html</u>. Accessed September 16, 2006.

143. Donabedian A. 1985. <u>Explorations in Quality Monitoring and Assessment and Monitoring – Volume III, The Methods and Findings of Quality Assessment and Monitoring: An Illustrated Analysis.</u> Health administration Press, Ann Arbor, MI.

144. Douglas CH, Higgins A, Dabbs, C, Walbank M. 2004. Health impact assessment for the sustainable futures of Salford. *J Epidemiol Community Health* 58: 642-648.

145. Dowd S, Davidhizar R. 1997. Change management – organizational culture as change factor. *Administrative Radiology Journal* 16:20-5.

146. Drake D, Fitzgerald S, Jaffe M. 1993. Hard Choices—Health Care at What Cost? Andrews & McMeel: Kansas City.

147. Droste TM. 1996. Merging corporate cultures in integrated systems. *Medical Network Strategy Report* 5:1-3.

148. Dwore, RB Dwore RB, Murray BP. 1989. Turnover at the top: Utah hospital CEOs in a turbulent era. *Hosp Health Serv Admin* Fall, 34(3): 333-351.

149. Dyer, Jr. WG: The Cycle of Cultural Evolution in Organizations, pages 200-229. In: Kilmann RH, Saxton MJ, Serpa R, et al (1985) Gaining Control of the Corporate Culture. San Franciso: Jossey-Bass.

150. Dyer, WG. 1987. Team building: Issues and alternatives (2nd ed.). Reading, MA: Addison Wesley Publishing Company.

151. Edmondson AC. 1996. "Learning from mistakes is easier said that done: Group and organizational influences on the detection and correction of human error." *Journal of Applied Behavioral Science* 32(1): 5-28.

152. Edmondson, AC. 2008. "The Competitive Imperative of Learning." Harvard Business Review July-August: 60-67.

153. Ellis SG, Weintraub W, Holmes D, Shaw R, Block PC, King SB. 1997. Relation of Operator Volume and Experience to Procedural Outcome of Percutaneous Coronary Revascularization at Hospitals With High Interventional Volumes. *Circulation* 95: 2479–84.

154. Engstrom P. 1995. Cultural differences can fray the knot after MDs, hospitals exchange vows. *Medical Network Strategy Report* 4:1-5.

155. Eubanks P. 1991. Identifying your hospital's corporate culture. *Hospitals* 65:46.

156. European Observatory on Health Care Systems 2000. Health Care Systems in Transition: Belgium. Copenhagen: World Health Organization. Accessed on February 10, 2006 at: http://www.euro.who.int/document/e71203.pdf.

157. Evans M. October 18, 2004. For a limited time only. *Modern Healthcare.* 34 (42): 6-8.

158. Feldstein PJ. 2005. *Health Care Economics*, 6th ed. Thomson Delmar Learning. Clifton, NY. Pp. 207-208.

159. Fennell ML, Alexander J. September 1987. "Organization boundary spanning and institutionalized environments." *Academy of Management Journal* 30: 456-476

160. Ferlie E, Fitzgerald L, Wood M. 2000. Getting evidence into clinical practice: an organizational behavior perspective. *Journal of Health Services Research & Policy* 5(2): 96-102.

161. Ferlie EB, Shortell SM. 2001. Improving the quality of health care in the United Kingdom and the United States: A framework for change. *Millbank Quarterly* 79(2): 281-315.

162. Ferrara-Love R. 1997. Changing organizational culture to implement organizational change. *Journal of Perianesthesia Nursing* 12: 12-6.

163. Fickeisen DH. Winter 1991. Learning How to Learn, An Interview with Kathy Greenberg. The Learning Revolution (IC#27) by the Context Institute. Page 42. www.context.org/ICLIB/IC27/Greenbrg.htm. Accessed December 2004.

164. Fiol CM, O'Connor EJ, Aguinis. 2001. All for one and one for all? The development and transfer of power across organizational levels. *Academy of Management Review*, 26(2): 224-242.

165. Fitzgerald FS. 1936. The Crack-Up. New Directions Books: New York. Reprinted 1945.

166. Flowers VS, Hughes CL. July/August 1973. Why employees stay. *Harvard Business Review* pp. 49-60.

167. Fletcher B, Jones F. 1992. Measuring Organizational Culture: The Cultural Audit. *Managerial Auditing Journal* 7 (6): 30-6.

168. Forrester JW. 1971. The counterintuitive behavior of social systems. *Technology Review* 73(3): 52-68.

169. Franczyk A. 2000. Turnover in hospital CEOs brings change to healthcare industry. *Business First.* Buffalo: Jul24, 2000. Vol 12, Iss. 44, pp1-2.

170. Freiberg K, Freiberg J. 1996. Nuts! Southwest Airlines' Crazy Recipe for Business and Personal Success. Broadway Books: New York.

171. Galloro V. February 19, 2001. Staffing outlook grim-High turnover expected to continue in skilled nursing, assisted living. *Modern Healthcare* 31(8): 64.

172. Garside P. 1998. Organizational context for quality: Lesson from the fields of organizational development and change management. *Quality in Health Care* 7(Suppl): S8-15

173. Garson A. 2001. The Edgar Mannheim Lecture: From white teeth to heart transplants: evolution in international concepts of the quality of healthcare. *Cardiology in the Young* 11: 601-608.

174. Gentry WD, Parkes KR. 1982. Psychologic stress in the intensive care unit and non-intensive unit nursing: A review of the past decade. *Heart & Lung* 11(1): 43-47

175. George JM, Jones GR. 1996. The experience and work and turnover intentions: Interactive effects of value attainment, job satisfaction, and positive mood. *Journal of Applied Psychology* 81(3): 318-325.

176. Gerowitz M, Lemieux-Charles L, Heginbothan C, ans Johnson B. 1996. Top Management Culture and Performance in Canadian, UK and US Hospitals. *Health Services Management Research* 6 (3): 69-78.

177. Glaser S, Zamanou S, Hacker K. 1987. Measuring and Interpreting Organizational Culture. *Management communication quarterly* 1 (2): 173-98.

178.   Glazner L. 1992. Understanding corporate cultures: use of systems theory and situational analysis. *AAOHN Journal* 40:383-7.

179.   Goldman RL. 1992. The reliability of peer assessment of quality of care. *JAMA* 267(7): 958-960.

180.   Goldman DP, McGlynn EA. 2005. U.S. Health Care: Facts about Cost, Access and Quality. Rand Report CP484.1. Accessed December 29, 2006 at: www.rand.org/pubs/corporate-pubs/CP484.1.

181.   Goldratt E, Cox J (1984). The Goal-A Process of Ongoing Improvement. North River Press, Great Barrington, MA.

182.   Goldsmith J. 2003. Digital Medicine: Implications for Healthcare Leaders. Chicago: Health Administration Press.

183.   Goodman EA, Boss RW. 1999. Burnout dimensions and voluntary and involuntary turnover in a health care setting. *Journal of Health & Human Services Administration* Spring, 21(4): 462-471.

184.   Goodman JM, Jones GR. 1996. The experience and work and turnover intentions: Interactive effects of value attainment, job satisfaction, and positive mood. *Journal of Applied Psychology* 81(3): 318-325.

185.   Goold M, Campbell A. 2002. Do you have a well-designed organization?" *Harvard Business Review* March 117-124.

186.   Gordon GG: "The Relationship of Corporate Culture to Industry Sector and Corporate Performance" pages 103-125. In: Kilmann RH, Saxton MJ, Serpa R, et al (1985) Gaining Control of the Corporate Culture. San Franciso: Jossey-Bass.

187.   Gray AM, Phillips VL, Normand C. 1996. The costs of nursing turnover: Evidence from the British National Health Service. *Health Policy* 38: 117-128

188.   Greco PJ, Eisenberg JM. 1993. Changing Physicians' Practices. *New England Journal of Medicine* 329(17): 1271-1274

189.   Greene J. February 6, 1995. Clinical integration increases profitability, efficiency—study. Modern Healthcare, page 39

190.   Griffeth RW, Hom PW, Hall TE. 1981. "How to estimate employee turnover costs. Personnel 58(4): 43-52.

191.   Griffeth RW, Hom PW. 2001. Retaining Valued Employees. Sage Publications, Thousand Oaks, CA.

192.   Groupman J. 2007. How Doctors Think. Houghton Miflin: New York.

193.   Grout JR. 2003. Preventing medical errors by designing benign failures. *Joint Commission Journal on Quality and Safety* 29(7): 354-362.

194.   Gustafson BM. 2001. Improving staff satisfaction ensures PFS success. *Healthcare Financial Management* 55(7): 66-68.

195.   Hadley J, Mitchell JM, Sulmasy DP, Bloch MG. 1999. Perceived financial incentives, HMO market penetration, and physicians' practice styles and satisfaction. *Health Services Research* Vol. 34, #1, Part II: 307-321

196.   Hale C. May 7, 2003. NHS Chiefs 'forced into trickery.' *The [London] Times*, P 6.

197. Hall ET, Hall MR. 1990. Understanding Cultural Differences. Intercultural Press, Yarmouth, Maine.

198. Hammer M, Champy J. 1994. Reengineering the Corporation-A Manifesto for Business Revolution. HarperBusiness, New York, NY.

199. Hammer M. 2001. The Agenda. Crown Business, New York.

200. Hannan, EL, Racz M, Kavey R-E, et al. 1998. Pediatric Cardiac Surgery: The Effect of Hospital and Surgeon Volume on In-hospital Mortality. *Pediatrics* 101(6): 963-69.

201. Hariri S, Prestipino AL, Rubash HE. April 2007. The Hospital-Physician Relationship: Past, Present and Future. *Clinical Orthopaedics and Related Research* 457: 78-86.

202. Harrison, R. 1972. Understanding Your Organization's Character. *Harvard Business Review* 5 (3): 119-28.

203. Hart LG, Robertson DG, Lishner DM, Rosenblatt RA. 1993. CEO turnover in rural northwest hospitals. *Hosp Health Serv Admin* Fall; 38(3): 353-374.

204. Hatch AP. 2005. CBS abandons Murrow Ideals. *Albuquerque Journal* October 20; Page A13.

205. Hawkes, Nigel. January 18, 2002. Patients get power to select surgeons. *London Times*

206. Heinlein, R.1966. The Moon Is A Harsh Mistress. Berkley Publishing Corp: New York.

207. Henninger D. January 10, 2003. "Marcus Welby doesn't live here anymore." *Wall Street Journal*, Page A10

208. Herzberg F. 1968. One more time: How do you motivate employees? *Harvard Business Review* Reprint RO301F in *Best of HBR* January 2003 pp. 3-11.

209. Herzlinger RE. 1997. Market-Driven Health Care. Addison-Wesley Publ., Reading MA.

210. Herzlinger RE. November 26, 2003. Back in the U.S.S.R. *Wall Street Journal*, Opinion, Vol 240, A16

211. Heskett JL, Sasser WE, Schlesinger LA: The Service Profit Chain, Free Press, NY, 1997.

212. Hill LD, Madara JL. November 2, 2005. Role of the Urban Academic Medical Center in US Health Care. *JAMA* 294(17): 2219-2220.

213. Hilts PJ. June 23, 1993. Health-care Chiefs' pay rises at issue." *New York Times*, pg D2.

214. Hoban CJ. 2002. From the lab to the clinic: Integration of pharmacogenics into clinical development. *Pharmacogenics* 3(4): 429-436. .

215. Hock D. 1999. Birth of the Chaordic Age. Berrett-Koehler: San Francisco.

216. Hofstede G, Neuijen B, Ohayv DD, Sanders G. 1990. Measuring organizational cultures: A qualitative and quantitative study across twenty cases." *Administrative Science Quarterly* 35:286-316.

217. Howard PK. July 31, 2002. There is no 'right to sue'. *Wall Street Journal*, Page 13.

218. Hughes L. 1990. Assessing organizational culture: Strategies for external consultant. *Nursing Forum* 25 (1): 15-19.

219. Hume SK. 1990. Strengthening the corporate culture. *Health Progress* 71:15-6, 19.

220. Huselid MA, Jackson SE, Schuler RS. 1997. Technical and strategic human resource management effectiveness as determinants of firm performance. *Academy of Management Journal* 40(1): 171-188.

221. Hutchinson J, Runge W, Mulvey M, et al. 2004. *Burkholderia cepacia* infections associated with intrinsically contaminated ultrasound gel: The role of microbial degradation of parabens. *Infection Control and Hospital Epidemiology* 25: 291-296

222. Iglehart J. 1998. Forum on the future of academic medicine: Session III—Getting from Here to There. *Academic Medicine* 73 (2): 146-151

223. Ingersoll GL, Kirsch JC, Merk SE, Lightfoot J. 2000. Relationship of Organizational culture and Readiness for Change to Employee Commitment to the Organization. *Journal of Nursing Admin* 30 (1); 11-20.

224. Irvine DM, Evans MG. 1995. Job satisfaction and Turnover among nurses: Integrating research findings across studies. *Nursing Research* July/August 44(4): 246-253.

225. Jacobs DC. 2004. A pragmatist approach to integrity in business ethics. *Journal of Management Inquiry September* 13(3): 215-223.

226. Jain KK. 2005. Personalised medicine for cancer: from drug development into clinical practice. *Expert Opin. Pharmacother.* 6(9): 1463-1476.

227. Janssen PPM, de Jonge J, Bakker AB. 1999. Specific determinants of intrinsic work motivation, burnout and turnover intentions: a study among nurses. *Journal of Advanced Nursing* 29(6): 1360-1369.

228. Jenkins KJ, Gauvreau K, Newburger JW, et al. 2002. Consensus-based method for risk adjustment for surgery for congenital heart disease. *Journal of Thoracic & Cardiovascular Surgery* January 123: 110-118.

229. Jha AK, Perlin JB, Kizer KW, Dudley RA. May 29, 2003. Effect of the transformation of the Veterans Affairs Health Care System and the quality of care. *New England Journal of Medicine* 348(2): 2218-2227.

230. Jiang HJ, Friedman B, Begun JW. 2006. Factors Associated with High-Quality/Low-Cost Hospital Performance. *Journal of Health Care Finance* Spring: 39-51

231. Johnson DE. 1997. Medical group cultures pose big challenges. *Health Care Strategic Management* 15:2-3.

232. Johnson J, Billingsley M. 1997. Reengineering the corporate culture of hospitals." *Nursing & Health Care Perspectives* 18:316-21.

233. Johnson L. 1999. Cutting costs by managing turnover. *Balance, The Journal of the American College of Health Care Administrators.* Sept/Oct 1999 pp 21-23.

234. Johnson, Rep. Nancy. February 2001. Congressional Outlook: Nursing Shortages. *Hospital Outlook* 4(2): 7

235. Johnson S. 2001. <u>Emergence.</u> New York: Simon & Schuster, 2001.

236. Joiner KA, Wormsley S. March 2005. Strategies for Defining Financial Benchmarks for the Research Mission in Academic Health Centers. *Academic Medicine* 80(3): 211-217.

237. Joiner KA. March 2005. A Strategy for allocating central funds to support new faculty recruitment. *Academic Medicine* 80(3): 218-224.

238. Joiner KA. July 2004. Sponsored-Research Funding by Newly Recruited Assistant Professors: Can It Be Modeled as a Sequential Series of Uncertain Events? *Academic Medicine* 79(7): 633-643.

239. Joiner KA. July 2004. Using Utility Theory to Optimize a Salary Incentive Plan for Grant-Funded Faculty, *Academic Medicine* 79(7): 652-660.

240. Jollis JG, Peterson ED, DeLong ER, et al. 1994. The Relation Between the Volume of Coronary Angioplasty Procedures at Hospitals Treating Medicare Beneficiaries and Short-Term Mortality. *New England Journal of Medicine* 331: 1625–29.

241. Jones WT. 1961. The Romantic Syndrome: Toward a new method in cultural anthropology and the history of ideas. The Hague: Martinus Wijhaff.

242. Jones CB. 1990a. Staff nurse turnover costs: Part I, a conceptual model. *Journal of Nursing Administration,* 20(4): 18-22. AND

243. Jones CB. 1990b. Staff nurse turnover costs: Part II, measurement and results. *Journal of Nursing Administration,* 20(5): 27-32.

244. Jones CB. 1992. Calculating and Updating Nursing Turnover Costs." *Nursing Economic$* January/February 10(1): 39-45, 78

245. Jones KR, DeBaca V, Yarbrough M. 1997. Organizational culture assessment before and after implementing patient-focused care. *Nursing Economics* 1997; 15:73-80.

246. Jones WJ. 2000. The 'Business' – or 'Public Service'—of Healthcare. *J Healthcare Mgmt* 45(5): 290-293

247. Jorgensen A: "Creating changes in the corporate culture: case study." *AAOHN Journal* 1991; 39:319-21.

248. Jung CG. 1973. Four archetypes: Mother/Rebirth/Spirit/Trickster. Princeton University Press: Princeton, NJ.

249. Jurkiewicz CL, Knouse SB, Giacalone RA (March/April 2001) "When an employee leaves: The effectiveness of clinician exit interviews and surveys." *Clinical Leadership Management Review* 15(2): 81-84.

250. Kaiser Family Foundation, March 2009. Health Care Costs – A Primer. Accessed March 2009 at: www.kff.org.

251. Kan JS, White RI, Mitchell SE, Gardner TJ. 1982. Percutaneous balloon valvuloplasty: a new method for treating congenital pulmonary valve stenosis. *New Engl J Med* 307: 540-542.

252. Kallestad B. Fall 2006. *Leadership Quarterly,* Associated Press Report accessed January 1, 2007 at: http://news.yahoo.com/s/ap/bad_bosses

253. Karcz A, Korn R, Burke MC, et al. (1996) Malpractice Claims Against Emergency Physicians in Massachusetts: 1975-1993. *Am J Emergency Medicine* 14: 341-345.

254. Kauffman, Draper. 1980. <u>Systems One: An Introduction to Systems Thinking</u>. SA Carlton, Minneapolis, MN.

255. Kauffman SA. 1995. <u>At Home in the Universe</u>. Oxford University Press, New York

256. Keeler EB, Brook RH, Goldberg GA, Kamberg CJ, Newhouse JP (1985) "How free care reduced hypertension in the Health Insurance Experiment." *JAMA* Oct. 11, 1985; Vol. 254: 1926-1931.

257. Keeton WP, Dobbs DB, Keeton RE, Owen DG. 1984. *Prosser and Keeton on The Law of Torts*. Fifth Edition. West Publishing Co., St. Paul, MN.

258. Kellerman B. 2007. What every leader needs to know about followers. *Harvard Business Review* December, pp. 84-91.

259. Kerr S. 1975. On the folly of rewarding A While hoping for B. *Academy of Mgmt Journal* 18: 769-783.

260. Kesner KA, Calkin JD. 1986. Critical care nurses' intent to stay in their positions. *Research in Nursing & Health* 9: 3-10.

261. Kessler DP, McClellan MB. 2002. How liability law affects medical productivity. *J Med Economics* 21(6): 931-955.

262. Kiel JM. 1998. Using data to reduce employee turnover. *Health Care Supervisor* 16(4): 12-19.

263. Kilmann RH, Saxton MJ, Serpa R, et al. 1985. <u>Gaining Control of the Corporate Culture</u>. San Franciso: Jossey-Bass. See: Kilmann RH: "Five Steps of Closing Culture Gaps" pages 351-369 and Kilmann RH, Saxton MJ and Serpa R: "Conclusion: Why Culture Is Not Just a Fad" pages 421-432.

264. Kinard J, Little B. 1999. Are hospitals facing a critical shortage of skilled workers? *Health Care Supervisor* 17(4): 54-62.

265. Kissick WL. 1995. Medicine and Management. Bridging the cultural gaps. *Physician Executive* 21:3-6.

266. Kite M. June 03, 2003. Fat people will have to diet if they want to see the doctor. *London Times*.

267. Klaasen P. March 14, 2007. Accessed at: www.cnn.com/2007/HEALTH/04/04/uninsured.dead.ap/index.html

268. Klein LW, Schaer GL, Calvin JE, et al. 1997. Does Low Individual Operator Coronary Interventional Procedural Volume Correlate with Worse Institutional Procedural Outcome? *Journal of the American College of Cardiology* 30, no. 4: 870–77.

269. Klienke JD. 1998. <u>Bleeding Edge-The Business of Health Care in the New Century</u>. Aspen Publishers, Gaithersburg, MD

270. Klienke JD. September/October 2005. Dot-Gov: Market failure and the creation of a national health information technology system. *Health Affairs* 24(5): 1246-1262.

271. Klingle RS, Burgoon M, Afifi W, Callister M. 1995. Rethinking how to measure organizational culture in the hospital setting. The Hospital Culture Scale. *Evaluation & the Health Professions* 18:166-86.

272. Kosmoski KA, Calkin JD. 1986. Critical care nurses' intent to stay in their positions. *Research in Nursing & Health* 9: 3-10.

273. Kotter JP, Schlesinger LA. 1979. Choosing strategies for change." *Harvard Business Review Mar*-Apr 57(2): 106-114

274. Kotter JP, Heskett JL. 1992. Corporate Culture and Performance. Free Press: New York.

275. Kouzes JM, Posner BZ. 1997. The Leadership Challenge; Jossey-Bass Inc., San Francisco

276. Krackhardt D, Porter LW. 1985. When friends leave: A structural analysis of the relationship between turnover and stayers' attitudes. *Administrative Science Quarterly*, 30, 42-61.

277. Kraman SS, Hamm G. 1999. Risk management: Extreme honesty may be the best policy. *Ann Int Med* 131(12): 963-967.

278. Kravitz RL, Rolph JE, Petersen L. 1997. Omission-Related Malpractice Claims and the Limits of Defensive Medicine. *Medical Care Research and Review* 54: 456-471.

279. Krauthammer C. 1998. Driving the best doctors away. *Washington Post* January 9; p A21.

280. Kubler-Ross, E. 1969. On Death and Dying. Touchstone: New York.

281. Lacour-Gayet F, Clarke D, Jacobs J, et al and the Aristotle Committee. 2004. The Aristotle Score: a complexity-adjusted method to evaluate surgical results. *European Journal of Cardio-Thoracic Surgery* 25: 911-924.

282. Landis SE. January 3, 2006. Do the Poor deserve life support? Accessed December12, 2006 at www.slate.com/toolbar.aspx?action.

283. Landon BE, Reschovsky J, Blumenthal D. 2003. Changes in career satisfaction among primary care and specialist physicians, 1997-2001. *JAMA* 289(4): 442-449.

284. Landro, Laura. December 22, 2003. Six prescriptions for what's ailing U.S. Health care. *Wall Street Journal* Vol 242 #122, pp. A1 & A10.

285. Langer E. 1997. The Power of Mindful Learning. Perseus Books: New York.

286. Langwell KM, Werner JL. 1984. Regional Variations in the Determinants of Professional Liability Claims. *Journal of Health Politics, Policy and Law* 9:475-88.

287. Laurance J. December 6, 2004. NHS Revolution: nurses to train as surgeons. *The Independent* (London)

288. Lawry TC. May 1995. Making culture a forethought. *Health Progress* 76(4): 22-25, 48

289. Lazlo E. 1972. The Systems View of the World. George Braziller, New York.

290. Leape LL. December 21, 1994. Error in Medicine. *JAMA* 272(3): 1851-1857

291. Lee RT, Ashforth BE. 1996. A meta-analytic examination of the correlates of the three dimensions of job burnout. *Journal of Applied Psychology* 81: 123-133.

292. Lerner J. 1997. *The Rush Initiative for Mediation of Medical Malpractice Claims.* 11 CBA Record 40.

293. Levering R, Moskovitz M. 1993. *The 100 Best Companies to Work for in America*, Doubleday, New York.

294. Levinson W, Roter DL, Mullooly JP, Dull VT, Frankel RM. 1997. Physician-Patient Communication: The Relationship with Malpractice Claims Among Primary Care Physicians and Surgeons. *JAMA* 277: 553-559.

295. Levitt S, Dubner S. 2005. <u>Freakonomics – A Rogue Economist Explores the Hidden Side of Everything</u>. Harper Collins: New York.

296. Lewin K. 1947. Frontiers in group dynamics. *Human Relations*, Volume 1, pp. 5-41

297. Linn A. February 12, 2005. Biggest Airbus Jet is Too Big. *Albuquerque Journal*, No. 43, C-1. 4

298. Lisney B, Allen C. 1993. Taking a snapshot of cultural change. *Personnel Management* 25 (2): 38-41.

299. Litwinenko A, Cooper CL: "The impact of trust status on corporate culture." *Journal of Management in Medicine* 1994; 8:8-17.

300. Localio AR, Lawthers AG, Brennan TA, et al. 1991. Relation between malpractice claims and adverse events due to negligence: Results of the Harvard Medical Practice Study III. *N Engl J Med* 325: 245-251.

301. Loop FD. 2001. On medical management. *J Thorac Cardiovasc Surg* 121(4): S25-S28.

302. Lorsch JW: "Strategic Myopia: Culture as an Invisible Barrier to Change" pages 84-102. In: Kilmann RH, Saxton MJ, Serpa R, et al (1985) <u>Gaining Control of the Corporate Culture</u>. San Franciso: Jossey-Bass.

303. Louis MR: "Sourcing Workplace Cultures: Why, When, and How" pages 126-136-102. In: Kilmann RH, Saxton MJ, Serpa R, et al (1985) <u>Gaining Control of the Corporate Culture</u>. San Franciso: Jossey-Bass.

304. Luft HS, Bunker, Enthoven AC. 1979. Should operations be regionalized? The empirical relation between surgical volume and mortality. *N Engl J Med* Dec 20; 301(25): 1364-69.

305. Luft, HS. 2003. From observing the relationship between volume and outcome to making policy recommendations – Comments on Sheikh. *Medical Care* 41(10): 1118-1122.

306. Lurie N, Manning WG, Peterson C, Goldberg GA, Phelps CA, Lilliard L. 1987. Preventive Care: Do we Practice what we preach? *American Journal of Public Health* 77:801-804.

307. Maarse H, Paulus A. Has solidarity survived? A comparative analysis of the effect of social health insurance reform in four European countries. *J Health, Politics, Policy and Law* 2003; 28(4): 585-614.

308. Machiavelli N. 1513. <u>The Prince</u>. Wordsworth Editions, Hertfordshire, England, 1993.

309. Mackenzie S. 1995. "Surveying the organizational culture in a NHS trust." *J Mgmt Med* 9(6): 69-77.

310. Maclean, N. 1992. <u>Young Men and Fire</u>. University of Chicago: Chicago.

311. Mahony L, Sleeper LA, Anderson PAW, et al. 2006. Pediatric Heart Network: A primer for the conduct of multicenter studies in children with congenital & acquired heart disease. *Pediatric Cardiology* 27: 191-198.

312. Malcolm L, Wright L, Barnett, Hendry C. 2003. Building a successful partnership between management and clinical leadership: experience from New Zealand. *British Medical Journal* 326: 653-654. Downloaded 31 August 2006 from doi:10.1136/bmj.326.7390.653.

313. Mann EE, Jefferson KJ. "Retaining staff: Using turnover indices and surveys. *JONA* 1988; 18(7,8): 17-23.

314. Mano-Negrin R (2001) "An occupational preference model of turnover behavior: The case of Israel's medical sector employees." *Journal of Management in Medicine* 15(2): 106-114.

315. Marmot M. 2004. The Status Syndrome – How Social Standing Affects Our Health and Longevity. Holt & Co.: New York.

316. Marsh R Mannari H. 1977. Organizational commitment and turnover: A predictive study. *Administrative Science Quarterly* 22: 57-75.

317. Martin, N. June 4, 2007. "Smokers who won't quit denied surgery" by Nicole Martin in the *Daily Telegraph Today*, June 4, 2007, at: http://www.telegraph.co.uk/global/ main.jhtml?xml=/global/2007/06/04/nhealth04.xml.

318. Martin TE. 1979. A contextual model of employee turnover intentions. *Academy of Management Journal* 22(2): 313-324.

319. Martin HJ: "Managing Specialized Corporate Cultures" pages 148-162. In: Kilmann RH, Saxton MJ, Serpa R, et al (1985) Gaining Control of the Corporate Culture. San Franciso: Jossey-Bass.

320. Maslow AH. 1943. A theory of human motivation. *Psychological Review* 50: 370-396.

321. Matus JC, Frazer GH. 1996. Job satisfaction among selected hospital CEOs." *The Health Care Supervisor* September 15(1): 41-60.

322. May L. 1993. Institutions and the transformation of personal values. Are the traditional values of caring and service in jeopardy? *Clinical Laboratory Management Review* 7:191-3.

323. Matus JC, Frazer GH. 1996. Job satisfaction among selected hospital CEOs. *The Health Care Supervisor* September 15(1): 41-60.

324. McCallum KL. May 7, 2001. All the good doctors always leave. Medical Economics 78(9): 55-6, 58, 61

325. McConnell CR. 1999. Staff turnover: Occasional friend, frequent foe, and continuing frustration. *Health Care Manager* 18(1): 1-13.

326. McDaniel RR. 1997. Strategic Leadership: A View from quantum and chaos theories. *Health Care Management Review* 22(1) 21-37.

327. McDaniel RR, Driebe DJ. 2001. Complexity Science and Health Care Management. *Advances in Health Care Management* 2: 11-36.

328. McFadden KL, Towell ER, Stock GN. 2004. Critical success factors for controlling and managing Hospital Errors. *Quality Management Journal* 2004; 11(1) 61-73.

329. McGinn R. May 10, 2006. Malpractice Caps Limit Care. *Albuquerque Journal*, #130, Page A11.

330. McGrath PD, Wennberg DE, Malenka DJ, et al. 1998. Operator Volume And Outcome in 12,998 Percutaneous Coronary Interventions. *Journal of American College of Cardiology* 31(3): 570–76.

331. McIntyre N, Popper KB. 1989. The critical attitude in medicine: the need for a new ethics. *British Medical Journal* 287:1919-1923

332. McMurray, AJ. 2003. The relationship between organizational climate and organizational culture. *Journal of the American Academy of Business*, 3: 1-8.

333. Melcher AJ (1976) Participation: A critical review of research findings. *Human Resource Management* Summer: 12-21.

334. Melville A. 1980. Job satisfaction in general practice: Implications for prescribing. *Social Sciences & Medicine* 14A(6): 495-499

335. Merry M. 1998. Will you manage your organization's culture, or will it manage you? *Integrated Healthcare Report* pp. 1-11.

336. Merry MD. 2004. What Deming Says. One of four essays on Can the gurus' concepts cure healthcare? In *Quality Progress* September pp. 28-30.

337. Meschievitz CS. 1994. Efficacious or Precarious? Comments on the Processing and Resolution of Medical Malpractice Claims in the United States, 3 Annals Health L. 123, 127-130.

338. Messinger DS, Bauer CR, Das A, et al. 2004. The maternal lifestyle study: Cognitive, motor, and behavioral outcomes of cocaine-exposed and opiate-exposed infants through three years of age. *Pediatrics* 113: 1677-168.

339. Metzloff TB. 1992. *Alternate Dispute Resolution Strategies in Medical Malpractice*. 9 Alaska L. Rev. 429, 431.

340. Metzloff TB. 1996. *The Unrealized Potential of Malpractice Arbitration*, 31 Wake Forest L. Rev. 203, 204, 1996 [reporting results from Henry S. Farber & Michelle J. White, *Medical Malpractice: An Empirical Examination of the Litigation Process*, 22 Rand J. Econ. 199 206 tbl.2 (1991)].

341. Metzloff TB. 1997. *Empirical Perspectives on Mediation and Malpractice*. 60-WTR Law & Contemp. Probs. 107, 110-113. *See also*, N.C. Gen. Stat. § 7A-38.1 (1998).

342. Millenson ML. 1999. <u>Demanding Medical Excellence: *Doctors and accountability in the Information Age*</u>. University of Chicago Press: Chicago.

343. Millenson, ML. 2003. The Silence. *Health Affairs* 22(2): 103-112.

344. Miller, J 1995. <u>Lockheed Martin's Skunk Works</u>. Midland Publishers: Leicester, England.

345. Miller RH, Lipton HL, Duke KS, Luft HS. 1996. Update Special Report, The San Diego Health Care System: A Snapshot Of Change. *Health Affairs* 15.1: 224-229.

346. Miller MM. December 25, 2003. Don't look for responsible leadership under tree. *Albuquerque Journal* Vol 358, A12

347. Miller WL, Crabtree BF, McDaniel R, Stange KC. May 1998. Understanding change in primary care practice using complexity theory. *Journal of Family Practice* 46(5): 369-376.

348. Mingardi A. November 17, 2006. A drug price path to avoid. *Albuquerque Journal*, A13.

349. Mintzberg H. 1983. <u>Structuring of Organizations</u>. Englewood Cliff: Prentice Hall.

350. Mirvis PH Lawler EE. 1977. Measuring the financial impact of employee attitudes. *Journal of Applied Psychology* 62:1-18.

351. Mitroff II and Kilmann RH: "Corporate Taboos and the Key to Unlocking Culture" pages 184-199. In: Kilmann RH, Saxton MJ, Serpa R, et al (1985) <u>Gaining Control of the Corporate Culture</u>. San Franciso: Jossey-Bass.

352. Mobley WH, Horner SO, Hollingsworth AT. 1978. Evaluation of precursors of hospital employee turnover. *Journal of Applied Psychology* 63(4): 408-414.

353. Mobley WH. 1982. <u>Employee Turnover: Causes, Consequences and Control</u>. Addison-Wesley, Reading, MA.

354. Moore WW. 1991. Corporate culture: modern day rites & rituals." *Healthcare Trends & Transition* 2:8-10, 12-3, 32-3.

355. Mosca L, Appel LJ, Benjamin EJ et al. 2004. Evidence-based guidelines for cardiovascular disease prevention in women. American Heart Association scientific statement. *Arterioscler Thromb Vasc Biol* Mar; 24(3): 29-50.

356. Mott DA. 2000. Pharmacist job turnover, length of service, and reasons for leaving, 1983-1997. *American Journal of Health-System Pharmacy* 57(10): 975-984.

357. Mowday RT, Steers RM, Porter LW. 1979. The measurement of organizational commitment. *Journal of Vocational Behavior* 14: 224-27.

358. Mowday RT. 1981. Viewing turnover from the perspective of those who remain: The relationship of job attitudes to attributions of the causes of turnover. *Journal of Applied Psychology* 66(1): 120-123.

359. Mullainathan S, Thaler RH. "Behavioral Economics." Accessed November 2006 at: http://introduction.behaviouralfinance.net/MuTh.pdf.

360. Mullaney, TJ. October 31, 2005. This Man Wants to Heal Health Care. *Business Weekly* 3957, p 74.

361. Naisbitt J. 1982. <u>Megatrends</u>. Warner Books: New York.

362. Neilsen DM. 2004. What Crosby says. One of four essays on Can the gurus' concepts cure healthcare? In *Quality Progress* September pp. 26-27

363. Nelson, Dave. October 2005. Baldrige – Just What The Doctor Ordered. *Quality Progress*, pp 69-75.

364. Neuhauser PC. 1999. Strategies for changing your corporate culture." [Comment on: *Frontiers of Health Services Management* Fall; 16(1): 3-29] *Frontiers of Health Services Management* 1999; 16:33-7.

365. Neumann E. 1955. The Great Mother: An analysis of archetype. Princeton, NJ: Princeton University Press.

366. NICE Manuals: Guide to the Methods of the Technology Appraisal. Accessed March 16, 2007 at: www.nice.org.uk.

367. Ocasio W, Kim H. 1999. The circulation of corporate control: Selection of functional backgrounds of new CEOs in large U.S. manufacturing firms. *Administrative Science Quarterly* 44(3): 532-563.

368. O'Connell C. 1999. A culture of change or a change of culture? *Nursing Administration Quarterly* 23:65-8.

369. O'Connor JP, Nash DB, Buehler ML, Bard M. 2002. Satisfaction higher for physician executives who treat patients, survey says. *The Physician Executive* May-June pp. 16-21

370. O'Daniell EE. 1999. Energizing corporate culture and creating competitive advantage: a new look at workforce programs. *Benefits Quarterly* 15:18-25.

371. Ogbrun PL, Julian TM, Brooker DC, et al. 1988. Perinatal Medical Negligence Closed Claims from the St. Paul Company, 1980-1982. *Journal of Reproductive Medicine* 33: 608-611.

372. O'leary, DS. 1988. Will a New Federal Climate Affect Joint Commission Confidentially Policy? *Joint Commission Perspectives* Septembre/Octobre 8. 9-10: 2-4.

373. Oliva R. 2002. Tradeoffs in response to work pressure in the service industry. *IEEE Engineering Management Review* First Quarter pp.53-62

374. Orentlicher D. 2000. Medical Malpractice: Treating the Causes Instead of the Symptoms. *Medical Care* 38: 247-249.

375. Osnos E. September 28, 2005. In China, health care is scalpers, lines, debt. *Chicago Tribune*, Section 1, pp 1 & 6.

376. Owen H. Winter 1991. Learning as Transformation. The Learning Revolution (IC#27) by the Context Institute. Page 42. www.context.org/ICLIB/IC27/Owen.htm. Accessed December 2004.

377. Pascale RT, Sternin J. 2005. Your Company's Secret Change Agents. *Harvard Business Rev.* 83(5): 73-81.

378. Pathman DE, Williams ES, Konrad TR. 1996. Rural physician satisfaction: its sources and relation to retention." *Journal of Rural Health* 12(5): 366-377.

379. Pathman DE, Konrad TR, Williams ES, et al. 2002. Physician job satisfaction, dissatisfaction, and turnover. *Journal of Family Practice* 51:593.

380. Patterson KJ and Wilkins AL: "You Can't Get There From Here: What Will Make Culture-Change Projects Fail" pages 262-291. In: Kilmann RH, Saxton MJ, Serpa R, et al (1985) Gaining Control of the Corporate Culture. San Franciso: Jossey-Bass.

381. Payne, J. April 9, 2007. Poor Getting Brushoff for Care. *Albuquerque Journal*, P. C1.

382. Pearson SD, Rawlins, MD. November 23/30, 2005. Quality, Innovation, and Value for Money: NICE and the British National Health Service. *JAMA* 294(20): 2618-2622.

383. Peirce JC. 2000. The paradox of physicians and administrators in health care organizations. *Health Care Management Review* 2(1): 7-28

384. Peters TJ, Waterman RH. 1982. In Search of Excellence. Warner Books, New York, NY

385. Petrock F. 1990. Corporate culture enhances profits." *HR Magazine* 35:64-6.

386. Pettigrew A. 1979. "On Studying Organizational Culture." *Administration Science Quarterly* 24:570-81.

387. Pettigrew A, Ferlie E, McKee L. 1992. Shaping Strategic Change-Making change in large organizations. The Case of the National Health Service. Sage Publ., London

388. Pfeffer J. April 1976. Beyond management and the worker: The Institutional Function of Management. *Academy of Management Review* 1(2): 36-46

389. Pfeffer J. 1994. Competitive Advantage Through People. Harvard Business School Press: Boston.

390. Pfeffer J, Sutton RI. 2000. The Knowing-Doing Gap. Harvard Business School Press, Boston, MA.

391. Phibbs CS, Bronstein JM, Buxton E, Phibbs RH. 1996. The Effects of Patient Volume and Level of Care at the Hospital of Birth on Neonatal Mortality. *Journal of the American Medical Association* 276: 1054–59.

392. Phillips RI. 1974. The informal organization in your hospital. *Radiologic Technology* 46(2): 101-106

393. Phillips K. August 16, 2005. Hospitals increasing tapping female executives. Nursezone.com. At: http://nursezone.com/include/PrintArticle.asp?articleid=12529.

394. Porter LW, Steers RM, Mowday RT. 1974. Organizational commitment, job satisfaction, and turnover among psychiatric technicians. *Journal of Applied Psychology* 59(5): 603-609.

395. Porter ME, Teisberg EO. 2006. Redefining Health Care – Creating Value-Based Competition on Results. Harvard Business School Publishing, Boston, MA.

396. Posner KL, Caplan RA, Cheney FW. 1996. Variation in Expert Opinion in Medical Malpractice Review. *Anesthesiology* 85: 1049-1054.

397. Prescott PA. 1986. Vacancy, stability, and turnover of registered nurses in hospitals. *Research in Nursing & Health* 9: 51-60.

398. Price JL, Mueller CW. 1981. A causal model of turnover for nurses. *Acad of Mgmt Journal* 24(3): 543-565.

399. Pritchard RD, Campbell KM, Campbell DJ. 1977. Effects of extrinsic financial rewards on intrinsic motivation. *Journal of Applied Psychology* 62(1): 9-15.

400. Proenca EJ. 1996. Market orientation and organizational culture in hospitals." *Journal of Hospital Marketing* 11:3-18.

401. Prosser WP, Dobbs DB, Keeton RE, Owen DG. 1984. Prosser and Keeton on The Law of Torts, Fifth Edition, West Publishing Cp: St Paul, MN.

402. Provan KG. July 1984. Interorganizational cooperation and decision making autonomy in a consortium multi-hospital system. *Academy of Management Review* 9(3): 494-504.

403. Quam L, Dingwall R, Fenn P. 1987. Medicine and the Law, Medical Malpractice in Perspective: I – The American Experience. *British Medical Journal* 294: 1529-1532.

404. Quigley W. December 17, 2001. London Report: Medical missteps compound in child's death. *Albuquerque Journal*, p A2

405. Quigley W. October 28, 2002. The health of health care. Quoting Martin Hickey, former Lovelace CEO. *Albuquerque Journal*, Outlook, pp. 3, 9

406. Quinn RE, Spreitzer GM. 1991. The Psychometrics of the competing values culture instrument and an analysis of the impact of organizational culture on quality of life. *Research in Organizational Change and Development,* 5:115-142.

407. Rabinowitz S, Hall DT. 1977. Organizational research on job involvement. *Psych Bull* 84:265-288.

408. Rasmussen, Tom. 29 July 2005. A Mandated Burden." The Wall Street Journal A-13.

409. Reno R. 2001. Health-care system is beyond repair. *Albuquerque Journal*, August 20. A8

410. Rentsch JR. 1990. Climate and culture: Interactions and qualitative differences in organizational meanings." *Journal of Applied Psychology*, 75, 668-681.

411. Richards BC, Thomasson G. 1992. Closed Liability Claims Analysis and the Medical Record. *Obstetrics & Gynecology* 80: 313-316.

412. Rickles D, Hawe P, Shiell A. 2007. A Simple guide to chaos and complexity. *J Epidemiol. Community Health* 61: 933-937, accessed November 20 2007 at: doi:10.1136/jech.2006.054254.

413. Riter RN. 1994. Changing organizational culture." *Journal of Long-term Care Administration* 22:11-13.

414. Roberts G. November 23, 2005. "Overweight patients to be denied NHS hip operations." *London Times*, Page 2.

415. Robinson s. 1981. Off the Wall at Callahan's. Tor Books, NY. Page 36.

416. Rogers EM. 1983. Diffusion of Innovation. The Free Press, New York.

417. Rosch E, Lloyd BB [eds.] (1978) Cognition and Categorization. Hillsdale, N.J.: Lawrence Erlbaum.

418. Rothermel RC. May 1993. "Mann Gulch Fire: A Race That Couldn't Be Won." Accessed March 2006 at: http://www.fs.fed.us/rm/pubs/int_gtr299.

419. Rousseau L. 1984. What are the real costs of employee turnover? *CA Magazine* (Toronto) 117(2): 48-55.

420. Rowley TJ. 1997. Moving beyond dyadic ties: A network theory of stakeholder influences. *Academy of Management Review*. 22: 887-910.

421. Rucci AJ, Kirn SP, Quinn RT. 1998. The employee-customer-profit chain at Sears. *Harvard Business Review* Jan/Feb, 83-97.

422. Sackett DL, Rosenberg WM, Gray JA, Haynes RB, Richardson WS. 1996. Evidence based medicine: what it is and what it isn't. *British Medical Journal* 312(7023): 71-2.

423. Sales, AL, Mirvis PH. 1984. When cultures collide: Issues in acquisition, in Managing Organizational Transitions by JR Kennedy, Publ: RD Irwin, Homewood, IL. pp. 107-133.

424. Sapienza AM: "Believing Is Seeing: How Culture Influences the Decisions Top Managers Make" pages 66-83. In: Kilmann RH, Saxton MJ, Serpa R, et al (1985) Gaining Control of the Corporate Culture. San Franciso: Jossey-Bass.

425. Sathe V: "How to Decipher and Change Corporate Culture" pages 230-261. In: Kilmann RH, Saxton MJ, Serpa R, et al (1985) Gaining Control of the Corporate Culture. San Franciso: Jossey-Bass.

426. Schein EH: "How culture forms, develops and changes," pages 17-43. In: Kilmann RH, Saxton MJ, Serpa R, et al (1985) Gaining Control of the Corporate Culture. San Franciso: Jossey-Bass.

427. Schelling TC. 1960. The Strategy of Conflict. Cambridge: Harvard University Press.

428. Schneider J. 1976. The "greener grass" phenomenon: Differential effects of a work context alternative on organizational participation and withdrawal intentions. *Organizational Behavior and Human Performance* 16: 308-33.

429. Schwartz WB, Komesar NK. 1978. Doctors, Damages and Deterrence. *New Engl J Med* 298: 1282-1289.

430. Schyve PM. 2004. What Feigenbaum says. One of four essays on "Can the gurus' concepts cure healthcare?" In *Quality Progress* September pp. 30-33.

431. Scott RA, Aiken LH, Mechanic D, Moravcsik J. 1995. Organizational aspects of caring. *Millbank Quarterly* 73(1): 77-95

432. Scott T, Mannion R, Davies H, Marshall M. 2003. The Quantitative Measurement of Organizational Culture in Health Care: A Review of the Available Instruments. *Health Services Research* 38(3): 923-38.

433. Seago J. 1997. Organizational Culture in Hospitals: Issues in Measurement. *Journal of Nursing Measurement* 5 (2): 165-78.

434. Senge PM. 1990. The Fifth Discipline-The Art and Practice of the Learning Organization. Currency Doubleday, New York.

435. Sfikas PM. 1998. Are Insurers Making Treatment Decisions? *JADA* 129: 1036-1039.

436. Shader K, Broome ME, Broome CD, West ME, Nash M. April 2001. Factors influencing satisfaction and anticipated turnover for nurses at an academic medical center. *Journal of Nursing Administration* 31(4): 210-216.

437. Shanahan MM. 1993. A comparative analysis of recruitment and retention of health care professionals. *Health Care Management Review* 18(3): 41-51.

438. Shanks H (1968) *The Art and Craft of Judging – The Decision of Learned Hand.* Macmillan Co., New York.

439. Shannon v. McNulty, M.D., 718 A.2d 828, (S.Ct.Pa. 1998) and Corporate Health Insurance, Inc. v. Texas Department of Insurance, 215 F.3d 526 (5thCir.2000) (rehearing den'd, 2000 WL 1035524) and Tex Civ. Prac. & Rem., § 88.001 et seq.; Tex. Ins. Code, art. 20A.09(e), 20A.12(a & b); 20A.12A, 28. 58A § 6(b & c), 28.58A § 6A, 21.58A § 8(f), 21.58C.

440. Shaw GB. 1913. *Preface to* The Doctor's Dilemma, Penguin: Baltimore. Reprinted in 1954.

441. Sheikh A, Hurwitz B. 1999. A national database of medical errors. *Journal of the Royal Society of Medicine* November 92: 554-555.

442. Sheikh, K. 2003. Reliability of provider volume and outcome associations for healthcare policy. *Medical Care* October, 41(10): 1111-1117.

443. Sherer JL. 1994. Corporate cultures. Turning 'us versus them' into 'we'." *Hospitals & Health Networks* 68:20-2, 24, 26-7.

444. Shortell SM. Fall 1988. The evolution of hospital systems: Unfulfilled promises and self-fulfilling prophecies. *Medical Care Review* 45: 745-772

445. Shortell SM, Gillies RR, Anderson DA, Mitchell JB, Morgan KL. Winter 1993. Creating organized delivery systems: The barriers and facilitators. *Hospital & Health Services Administration* 38(4): 447-466

446. Shortell SM, O'Brien JL, Carman JM, et al. June 1995. Assessing the impact of continuous quality improvement/total quality management: Concept versus implementation. *Health Services Research* 30(2): 377-401.

447. Shortell S. March 1997. Commentary on: "Physician-Hospital integration and the economic theory of the firm" by JC Robinson. *Medical Care Research and Review* 54:3-24.

448. Shortell SM, Bennett CL, Byck GR. 1998. Assessing the impact of continuous quality improvement on clinical practice: What it will take to accelerate progress. *Millbank Quarterly* 76(4): 593-624.

449. Shortell S, Waters T, Budetti P, Clarke K. 1998. Physicians as double agents: Maintaining trust in an era of multiple accountabilities. *JAMA* 23: 1102-1108.

450. Shortell SM, Gillies RR, Anderson DA, Morgan-Erickson K, Mitchell J. 2000. Remaking Health Care in America: The Evolution of Organized Delivery Systems. San Francisco: Jossey-Bass.

451. Shortell SM, Jones RH, Rademaker AW, et al. 2000. Assessing the Impact of Total Quality management and Organizational Culture on Multiple Outcomes of Care for Coronary Artery Bypass Graft Surgery Patients. *Medical Care* 38 (2): 207-17.

452. Shortell SM, Zazzali JL, Burns LR, et al. 2001. "Implementing Evidence-Based Medicine: The Role of Market Pressures, Compensation Incentives, and Culture in Physician Organization. *Medical Care* 39 (7, Supplement): I-62-78.

453. Shorter E. 1985. Bedside Manners. Simon & Schuster: New York

454. Sieveking N, Bellet W, Marston RC. 1993. Employees' view of their work experience in private hospitals. *Health Services Management Research* 6 (2): 129-38.

455. Simone JV. 1999. Understanding Academic Medical Centers: Simone's Maxims. *Clinical Cancer Research* 5:2281-2285

456. Simunovic M, To T, Theriault, M, et al. Pediatric Cardiac Surgery: The Effect of Hospital and Surgeon Volume on In-hospital Mortality. *Pediatrics* 1998; 101(6): 963-69.

457. Simons R, Davila A. 1998. "How high is your return on management? *Harvard Business Review* 76; 70-80

458. Smircich, L. 1985. Is the concept of culture a paradigm for understanding organizations and ourselves? In P. J. Frost, L. F. Moore, M. R. Louis, C. C. Lundberg, and J. Martin (Eds.), Organizational Culture (pp. 55-72). Beverly Hills, Calif.: Sage.

459. Smith B, West K. 2002. Death certification: an audit of practice entering the 21st century. *Journal of Clinical Pathology* 55: 275-279.

460. Smith GCS, Pell JP. 2003. Parachute use to prevent death and major trauma related to gravitational challenge: systematic review of randomized controlled trials. *British Medical Journal* 327: 1459-61.

461. Smith FJ. 1977. Work attitudes as predictors of attendance on a specific day. *Journal of Applied Psychology* 62(1): 16-19.

462. Smith HL, Yourstone S, Lorber D, Mann B. 2001. Managed care and medical practice guidelines: The thorny problem of attaining physician compliance. In Advances in Health Care Management, Vol II, Elsevier Science Ltd., New York, NY

463. Smith HL, Waldman JD, Fottler M, Hood JN. 2005. Strategic Management of Internal Customers: Building Value through Human Capital and Culture." *Journal of Nursing Administration* November, **In Press**

464. Soffel D, Luft HS. 1993. Anatomy of health care reform proposals. *Western Jrnl of Medicine* 159: 494-500.

465. Spear S, Bowen HK. 1999. Decoding the DNA of the Toyota Production system. *Harvard Business Review* September/October pp. 97-106.

466. Spear SJ. September 2005. Fixing Healthcare from the Inside, Today. *Harvard Business Review*, pp. 2-16.

467. Steel RP, Ovalle NK. 1984. A Review and meta-analysis of research on the relationship between behavioral intentions and employee turnover. *Journal of Applied Psychology* 69(4): 673-686.

468. Steiger B. Nov/Dec 2006. Survey Results: Doctors Say Morale Is Hurting. *Physician Executive*. Pp. 6-15. Accessed January 23, 2006 at: www.acpe.org/education/surveys/morale/morale.htm.

469. Sterman JD. 2002. Systems dynamics modeling: Tools for learning in a complex world. *IEEE Engineering Management Review* First Quarter pp. 42-52.

470. Sterman J. 2006. Learning from evidence on a complex world. *Amer Journal of Public Health* 96: 505-514.

471. Stevenson, K. 2000. Are your Practices Resistant to Changing Their Clinical Culture? *Primary Care Report* 2 (5): 19-20.

472. Stocking B. 1992. Promoting change in clinical care. *Quality in health care* 1: 56-60.

473. Stoller JK, Orens DK, Kester L. March 2001. The impact of turnover among respiratory care practitioners in a health care system: Frequency and associated costs. *Respiratory Care* 46(3): 238-242.

474. Stossel T, Shaywitz D. July 9, 2006. Biotech Bucks Don't Corrupt Researchers. Reprinted from the *Washington Post* in the *Albuquerque Journal*, Page B3.

475. Stowe JD. 2000. Staff turnover or staff retention: Understanding the dynamics of generations at work in the 21st century. *Canadian Veterinary Journal* 41(10): 803-808

476. Stross, C. 2004. The Family Trade. Tom Doherty Associates Books: New York.

477. Stubblefield A. 2005. The Baptist Healthcare Journey to Excellence, Wiley & Sons: Hoboken, NJ.

478. Studdert DM, Thomas EJ, Burstin HR, Orav J, Brennan TA. 2000. Negligent Care and Malpractice Claiming Behavior in Utah and Colorado. *Medical Care* 38: 250-260.

479. Studer, Q. 2003. Hardwiring Excellence. Gulf Breeze, FL. Fire Starter Publishing

480. Surowiecki J. 2004. The Wisdom of Crowds. Anchor Books: New York.

481. Swift B, West K. 2002. Death certification: an audit of practice entering the 21st century. *Journal of Clinical Pathology* 55: 275-279

482. Tai TWC, Bame SI, Robinson CD. 1998. Review of nursing turnover research, 1977-1996. *Soc. Sci. Med.* 47(12): 1905-1924.

483. Taragin MI, Wilczek AP, Karns ME, Trout R, Carson JL. 1992. Physician demographics and the risk of medical malpractice. *Amer J Med* 93: 537-542.

484. Taragin MI, Sonnenberg FA, Karns ME, Trout R, Shapiro S, Carson JL. 1994. Does Physician Performance Explain Interspecialty Differences in Malpractice Claim Rates? *Medical Care* 32: 661-667.

485. Thomas C, Ward M, Chorba C, Kumiega A (1990) "Measuring and interpreting organizational culture." *Journal of Nursing Administration* 20(6): 17-24.

486. Thomas EJ, Studdert DM, Burstin HR, et al. 2000. Incidence and Types of Adverse Events and Negligent Care in Utah and Colorado. *Medical Care* 38: 261-271.

487. Thompson, Clive. December 10, 2006. Bicycle Helmets Put You At Risk. *The New York Times Magazine*, Section 6, Page 36.

488. Tribus M. 1992. The germ theory of management. *National Institute for Engineering Management & Systems*, Publication #1459

489. Tribus M. February 1992. Reducing Deming's 14 Points to practice. *Quality First*. National Institute for Engineering Management and Systems, NSPE Publication #1459

490. Trice HM, Beyer JM (1984) "Studying organizational cultures through rites and ceremonials." *Academy of Management Review* 9(4): 653-669.

491. Tucker R, McCoy W, Evans. 1990. Can questionnaires Objectively Assess Organizational Culture? *Journal of Managerial Psychology* 5 (4): 4-11.

492. Tuchman B. 1984. The March of Folly. Alfred Knopf: New York.

493. U.S. General Accounting Office (GAO). Impact on Hospital and Physician Costs Extends Beyond Insurance. *Medical Liability* 95.169 (1995): 01-17.

494. Uttal B (October 17, 1983) "The Corporate Culture Vultures." *Fortune* pp. 66-72.

495. Van der Merwe R, Miller S. 1971. The Measurement of Labour Turnover. *Human Relations* 24(3): 233-253

496. Van Watson GH. 2002. Peter F. Drucker: Delivering Value to Customers. *Quality Progress* May pp. 55-61.

497. Vergara GH. 1999. Finding a compatible corporate culture. *Healthcare Executive* 14:46-7.

498. Waldman JD, Young TS, Pappelbaum SJ, Turner SW, Kirkpatrick SE, George L. 1982. Pediatric cardiac catheterization with 'same-day' discharge. *Amer J Cardiol* 50:800-804.

499. Waldman JD, Pappelbaum SJ, George L, Lamberti JJ, Lodge FA. 1984. Cost-containment strategies in congenital heart disease. *West J Med* 141:123-126.

500. Waldman JD, Ratzan RM, Pappelbaum SJ. 1998. Physicians must abandon the *illusion* of autonomy.... *Pediatric Cardiology* 19:9-17.

501. Waldman JD. 2001. Aim with Echo in Pulmonary Atresia (The echo machine *works* in the cath lab.) *Pediatric Cardiology* 22(2): 91-92.

502. Waldman JD, McCullough G. 2002. A Calculus of *Unnecessary* Echocardiograms- Application of management principles to healthcare. *Pediatric Cardiology* 23: 186-191.

503. Waldman JD, Spector RA. 2003. Malpractice claims analysis yields widely applicable principles. *Pediatric Cardiology* 24(2): 109-117.

504. Waldman JD, Smith HL, Hood JN. 2003. Corporate Culture –The missing piece of the healthcare puzzle. *Hospital Topics* 81(1): 5-14.

505. Waldman JD, Schargel F. 2003. Twins in Trouble: The need for system-wide reform of both Healthcare and Education. *Total Quality Management & Business Excellence* October, 14(8): 895-901.

506. Waldman JD, Yourstone SA, Smith HL. 2003. Learning Curves in Healthcare. *Health Care Management Review* 28(1): 43-56.

507. Waldman JD, Smith HL, Kelly F, Arora S. 2004. The Shocking Cost of Turnover in Healthcare. *Health Care Management Review* 29(1): 2-7.

508. Waldman JD, Arora S. 2004. Retention rather than turnover—A Better and Complementary HR Method. *Human Resource Planning* 27(3): 6-9.

509. Waldman JD, Hood JN, Smith HL, Arora S, Herzon F, Lyford P. 2004. Changing the Approach to Workforce Movements: Application of Net Retention Rate. *Journal of Applied Business and Economics*. 24(2): 38-60.

510. Waldman JD, Schargel F. 2006. Twins in Trouble (II): Systems Thinking in Healthcare and Education. *Total Quality Management & Business Excellence* 17(1): 117-130.

189

511. Waldman JD, Arora S, Smith HL, Hood JN. 2006. Improving medical practice outcomes by retaining clinicians. *Journal of Medical Practice Management* March/April pp. 263-271.

512. Waldman JD. 2006. Change the Metrics: If *you get what you measure*, then measure what you want – retention." *Journal of Medical Practice Management* July/August, pp. 1-7.

513. Waldman JD, Hood JN, Smith HL. 2006. Healthcare CEO and Physician – Reaching Common Ground. *J of Healthcare Mgmt.* May/June 51(3): 171-187.

514. Waldman JD, Yourstone SA, Smith HL. 2007. Learning-*The* Means to Improve Medical Outcomes. *Health Services Mgmt Research* 2007; 20: 227-237.

515. Waldman JD, Smith HL. 2007. Thinking Systems need Systems Thinking. *Systems Research and Behavioral Science* 24: 1-15.

516. Waldman JD, Cohn K. September 2007. Mend the *Gap*. In The Business of Health, Editors: KH Cohn & D Hough, Praeger Perspectives, New York.

517. Waldman JD. 2009. The Triple Standard in Healthcare. *Calif J Politics & Policy* 1(1): 1-13.

518. Waldman JD, Smith HL. 2010. A Systems Approach to Medical Malpractice. *In Review.*

519. Walker J, Pan Eric, Douglas J, Adler-Milstein J, Bates DW, Middleton B. January 2005. The Value of Health Care Information Exchange And Interoperability. *Heath Affairs.* W 5—10-18.

520. *Wall Street Journal* Editorial, January 2, 2003. Lawyers vs. Patients---III, p. A14.

521. Wallach EJ. 1983. Individuals and organizations: The cultural match. *Training and Development Journal* 37: 29-36.

522. Walshe K, Rundall TG. 2001. Evidence-based management: From theory to practice in health care." *Millbank Quarterly* 79(3): 429-457

523. Ward CJ. 1991. Analysis of 500 obstetric and gynecologic malpractice claims: Causes and prevention. *Am J Obstet Gynecol* 165: 298306.

524. Watts, AW. 1951. The Wisdom of Insecurity. Pantheon Books: New York.

525. Watson GH. 2002. Peter F. Drucker: Delivering Value to Customers. *Quality Progress* May pp. 55-61.

526. Weber J, Wheelwright S. 1997. Massachusetts General Hospital: CABG Surgery (A). *Harvard Business School Case* # 9-696-015

527. Weick KE. 1993. The collapse of sensemaking in organizations: The Mann Gulch Disaster." *Administrative Science Quarterly* 38: 628-652.

528. Weil TP. 1987. The changing relationship between physicians and the hospital CEO. *Trustee* Feb; 40(2): 15-18.

529. Weil PA. 1990. Job turnover of CEOs in teaching and nonteaching hospitals. *Academic Medicine* 65(1): 1-7.

530. Weisman CS, Alexander CS, Chase GA. 1981. Determinants of hospital staff nurse turnover. *Medical Care* 19(4): 431-443.

531. <u>Wickline v. State</u>, 192 Cal. App.3d 16.0.1645 (1986), 239 Cal.Rptr. 805,825.

532. Wiener, Y. 1988. Forms of value systems: A focus on organizational effectiveness and cultural change and maintenance. *Academy of Management Review* 13: 534-545.

533. Wilcox FK. 1993. Corporate culture in a mythless society. *Amer Journal of Medical Quality* 1993; 8: 134-7.

534. Wilson CN, Meadors AC. 1990. Hospital Chief Executive Officer Turnover. *Hospital Topics* 68(1): 35-39

535. Wilson CN, Stranahan H. 2000. Organizational characteristics associated with hospital CEO turnover. *Journal of Health Care Management* 45(6): 395-404

536. Wilson L. July 22, 2004. Healthier habits will reduce medical costs. *Albuquerque Journal* A13.

537. Winton R, March 18, 2009. Former City of Angels hospital executive pleads guilty to paying kickbacks. Accessed March 2009 at: http://latimes.com/news/local/la-me-medfraud19-2009mar19,0,934741.story.

538. Wise LC. 1990. Tracking turnover. *Nursing Economics* 8(1): 45-51

539. Wittkower ED, Stauble WJ. 1972. Psychiatry and the general practitioner. *Psychiatry Med* 3:287-301.

540. Wood KM, Matthews GE. 1997. Overcoming the physician group-hospital cultural gap. *Healthcare Financial Management* 51:69-70.

541. Woolhandler S, Campbell T, Himmelstein DU. 2003. Costs of Health Care Administration in the United States and Canada. *NEJM* 349:768-775.

542. Wu AW, Cavanaugh TA, McPhee SJ, Lo B, Micco GP. 1997. To tell the truth – Ethical and Practical Issues in disclosing medical mistakes to patients. *J Gen Intern Med* 12: 770-775.

543. Wysocki B. April 9, 2004. To fix health care, hospitals take tips from factory floor. *Wall Street Journal* A6.

544. Yelle LE. 1979. The Learning Curve—Historical Review and Comprehensive Survey. *Decision Sciences* 302–28.

545. Yeung KO, Brockbank JW, Ulrich DO. 1991. Organizational culture and human resource practices: an empirical assessment. *Research in Organizational Change and Development* 5: 59-82.

546. Young GJ, Charns MP, Daley J, et al. Best Practices for Managing Surgical Services: The Role of Coordination. *Health Care Management Review* 1997; 22(4): 72-81.

547. Zammuto RF, Krakower JY. 1991. Quantitative and qualitative studies of organizational culture. *Res in Organizational Change and Development* 5:83-114.

548. Zimmerman R, Oster C. June 24, 2002. Insurers' missteps helped provoke malpractice 'crisis.' *Wall Street Journal*, pp 1, 8.

549. Zuger, A. 2004. Dissatisfaction with Medical Practice. *New England Journal of Medicine* 350(1): 69-76